Biography Today

*Profiles
of People
of Interest
to Young
Readers*

Volume 17
Issue 2
April 2008

e D. Abbey
aging Editor

*P.O. Box 31-1640
Detroit, MI 48231-1640*

Cherie D. Abbey, *Managing Editor*

Peggy Daniels, Laurie DiMauro, Joan Goldsworthy, Jeff Hill, Kevin Hillstrom, Laurie C. Hillstrom, Eve Nagler, and Diane Telgen, *Sketch Writers*

Allison A. Beckett and Mary Butler, *Research Staff*

* * *

Peter E. Ruffner, *Publisher*
Matthew P. Barbour, *Senior Vice President*

* * *

Elizabeth Collins, *Research and Permissions Coordinator*
Kevin M. Hayes, *Operations Manager*
Cherry Stockdale, *Permissions Assistant*

Shirley Amore, Martha Johns, and Kirk Kauffman, *Administrative Staff*

Contents

Preface

Biography Today is a magazine designed and written for the young read-er—ages 9 and above—and covers individuals that librarians and teachers tell us that young people want to know about most: entertainers, athletes, writers, illustrators, cartoonists, and political leaders.

The Plan of the Work

The publication was especially created to appeal to young readers in a for-mat they can enjoy reading and readily understand. Each issue contains approximately 10 sketches arranged alphabetically. Each entry provides at least one picture of the individual profiled, and bold-faced rubrics lead the reader to information on birth, youth, early memories, education, first jobs, marriage and family, career highlights, memorable experiences, hobbies, and honors and awards. Each of the entries ends with a list of easily acces-sible sources designed to lead the student to further reading on the indi-vidual and a current address. Retrospective entries are also included, writ-ten to provide a perspective on the individual's entire career.

Biographies are prepared by Omnigraphics editors after extensive research, utilizing the most current materials available. Those sources that are gener-ally available to students appear in the list of further reading at the end of the sketch.

Indexes

Cumulative indexes are an important component of *Biography Today*. Each issue of the *Biography Today* General Series includes a Cumulative Names Index, which comprises all individuals profiled in *Biography Today* since the series began in 1992. In addition, we compile three other indexes: the Cu-mulative General Index, Places of Birth Index, and Birthday Index. See our web site, www.biographytoday.com, for these three indexes, along with the Names Index. All *Biography Today* indexes are cumulative, including all indi-viduals profiled in both the General Series and the Subject Series.

Our Advisors

This series was reviewed by an Advisory Board comprising librarians, children's literature specialists, and reading instructors to ensure that the concept of this publication—to provide a readable and accessible biographical magazine for young readers—was on target. They evaluated the title as it developed, and their suggestions have proved invaluable. Any errors, however, are ours alone. We'd like to list the Advisory Board members, and to thank them for their efforts.

Our Advisory Board stressed to us that we should not shy away from controversial or unconventional people in our profiles, and we have tried to follow their advice. The Advisory Board also mentioned that the sketches might be useful in reluctant reader and adult literacy programs, and we would value any comments librarians might have about the suitability of our magazine for those purposes.

Your Comments Are Welcome

Our goal is to be accurate and up-to-date, to give young readers information they can learn from and enjoy. Now we want to know what you think. Take a look at this issue of *Biography Today*, on approval. Write or call me with your comments. We want to provide an excellent source of biographical information for young people. Let us know how you think we're doing.

Cherie Abbey
Managing Editor, *Biography Today*
Omnigraphics, Inc.
P.O. Box 31-1640
Detroit, MI 48231-1640

editor@biographytoday.com
www.biographytoday.com

Congratulations!

Congratulations to the following individuals and libraries who are receiving a free copy of *Biography Today*, Vol. 17, No. 2, for suggesting people who appear in this issue.

Bershard Horton, Longview, TX

Randy Olund, Carrington Middle School Media Center, Durham, NC

Lisa Scharf, Memorial Junior High School, Mentor, OH

Lisa Scharf, Ridge Junior High School, Mentor, OH

Bill Bass 1928-

American Forensic Anthropologist and Author
Pioneer in the Study of Human Decomposition

BIRTH

William Marvin Bass III was born on August 30, 1928, in
Staunton, Virginia. His birth father, William Marvin Bass Jr., was
a lawyer, and his mother, Jennie Bass, taught home economics.

YOUTH

One of the most important events of Bill Bass's young life occurred when he was very young. When he was just three years

old, his father committed suicide, perhaps upset over money-losing investments that he had made for some of his legal clients. "The instant he pulled the trigger, my father slipped from my grasp—slipped away from all of us," Bass later noted in his book *Death's Acre*, "and he remains out of reach to this day."

The loss of his birth father had a lasting influence on Bill. He believed it may have even been a factor in his later decision to choose a career in forensic anthropology. "I deal daily with death," Bass explained about his job, which involves the examination of human remains. "Perhaps when I grasp the bones of the dead, I'm somehow trying to grasp *him*, the one dead man who remains forever elusive." His mother later married his father's brother, Charles Bass, who was a geologist.

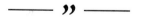

> *Bass's father committed suicide when he was very young, which had a profound effect on him. "I deal daily with death," he said about his job, which involves the examination of human remains. "Perhaps when I grasp the bones of the dead, I'm somehow trying to grasp* him, *the one dead man who remains forever elusive."*

EDUCATION

Bass lived in Stephens City, Virginia, during his youth and graduated from Stephens City High school in 1946. He earned a bachelor's degree in psychology from the University of Virginia in 1951 and then spent several years as a member of the U.S. Army during the Korean War. After leaving the service in 1953, he began a master's degree program at the University of Kentucky, planning to pursue a career as a college counselor. Bass began to have doubts about his chosen career, however, and came to realize that he "didn't want to talk to people with problems every day." As his interest in counseling faded, he became more interested in anthropology—the study of how humans have lived and developed—and took several classes in the subject.

One aspect of anthropological research involves osteology, the study of human bones, to understand more about the people of the past. These skills can also be used in criminal investigations and legal proceedings, because bone experts are able to obtain important information about a person who has died by looking at skeletal remains. People who specialize in this subject are known as forensic anthropologists. One of the professors

Bass studied with at the University of Kentucky, Dr. Charles E. Snow, was a well-known figure in the field of forensic anthropology.

One day in 1955, Snow asked Bass to assist him as he tried to identify the remains of a person who had been killed in a traffic crash. It was an experience that changed the young student's life. "Right there, I knew: that's what I wanted to do," Bass later explained. "It was fascinating to see the way burned and broken bones could identify a victim, solve a long-standing mystery, close a case. From that moment on, I decided, I would focus on forensics."

Bass received his master's degree in anthropology from the University of Kentucky in 1956 and then enrolled in the doctoral (PhD) program at the University of Pennsylvania. There, he studied with Wilton M. Krogman, a well-known pioneer of forensic anthropology who was known as "the bone detective." Bass graduated with a doctoral degree (PhD) in anthropology in 1961.

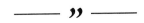

"Right there, I knew: that's what I wanted to do," Bass said about the first time he tried to identify someone who had been killed. "It was fascinating to see the way burned and broken bones could identify a victim, solve a long-standing mystery, close a case. From that moment on, I decided, I would focus on forensics."

CAREER HIGHLIGHTS

Initially, Bass focused on traditional anthropological studies—that is, studying people of the past rather than modern crimes. His first large-scale project grew out of a summer job that he had begun with the Smithsonian Institution in 1956, while he was still a student. That first year, he was based in Washington DC, where he analyzed the bones of Native Americans that had been unearthed from archaeological sites in the western United States. In 1957, he joined other archaeologists at a "dig" or excavation site in South Dakota. He was part of a large team that was working to uncover Native American artifacts before the area was submerged due to the construction of dams on the Missouri River. Bass made important contributions to unearthing historic burial sites in the area, and he continued his summertime work in South Dakota for 14 years.

Bass's career as a college educator began in 1960, when he took a temporary teaching assignment at the University of Nebraska. Later that year, he be-

came a member of the faculty at the University of Kansas and taught in the Department of Anthropology for 11 years. In 1971, he was named the head of the anthropology program at the University of Tennessee in Knoxville.

Forensic Anthropology

Bass began his work in forensic anthropology during his years in Kansas. Law enforcement officers would often contact him after a body had been discovered, and Bass would study the remains to discover important information. "When you examine a body in a forensic case," he explained, "the ultimate goal is to make a positive identification. If possible, you also want to determine the cause of death.... But before you can tell who someone is and how they died—and you won't always be able to tell—you start with the big four: sex, age, race, and stature."

By analyzing bones, a forensic anthropologist can answer these questions in various ways. For instance, the shape of pelvis bones can indicate if a person is male or female. The structure of the teeth and jaw can identify race. The manner in which the bones of the skull are joined indicate age. And the sizes of certain bones, such as the femur or thighbone, allow scientists to estimate the individual's height. In certain cases, more detailed information can be detected from skeletal remains. Damage to the bones may show how the person was killed, and the pattern of cavities in teeth can be matched to dental records to reveal the person's identity.

Bass continued to assist in law enforcement investigations after joining the University of Tennessee faculty. He was named the state forensic anthropologist, and, in that capacity, he frequently worked with police and sheriff's departments all over Tennessee. His expertise yielded useful information in a number of investigations, yet it was a much less satisfying case in 1977 that would inspire him to make an important professional breakthrough.

After examining the body of a man that had been found in the town of Franklin, Bass estimated that the person had died less than a year earlier, and the case became a well-publicized murder investigation. On further study, however, it was found that the body was actually that of a Civil War colonel who had been killed in a battle in 1864 and had been dislodged from his grave by looters. "I only missed it by 113 years!" Bass said of his incorrect estimate. Because the body had been embalmed (not a common practice in the mid-1800s) and well sealed in a cast-iron coffin, it was remarkably well preserved.

The problem was that Bass and other forensic anthropologists knew a lot about bones, but they had relatively little understanding of what happens to a body as it begins to decompose after death. "It made me realize how totally clueless we were about death," he said of the case involving the Civil War corpse. After puzzling over the problem for a time, Bass came up with a simple idea but one that would prove to be extremely important. "The only way to do it," he explained, "was to let a body rot and watch it."

> "When you examine a body in a forensic case, the ultimate goal is to make a positive identification," Bass explained. "If possible, you also want to determine the cause of death.... But before you can tell who someone is and how they died—and you won't always be able to tell—you start with the big four: sex, age, race, and stature."

Creating the "Body Farm"

In May 1981, Dr. Bass and several graduate students retrieved the body of 73-year-old man who had passed away several days before and whose remains had been donated to the university by his daughter. They took the corpse to a fenced parcel of land on the university campus and laid it on an outdoor concrete pad. Then they closed and locked the gate and left the body to decompose. So began the work of the University of Tennessee An-

Bass studying a body at the Body Farm.

thropology Research Facility, a place that would later become known by a more colorful name: "the Body Farm."

In the years since, hundreds of other corpses have likewise been studied at the site by Bass and his colleagues. Today, more than 25 years after that first study, the Body Farm is still the only facility of its kind in the world.

The idea of a "farm" filled with 20 to 40 decomposing bodies can be an upsetting thought for many people, but it has been a great asset for forensic anthropologists and law enforcement investigators. Determining the precise time that a death took place is extremely important in murder cases because it allows police to better understand what happened and to identify potential suspects. "The crime-scene people find a body in the woods," Bass explained, "and the first thing they want to know is, 'When did he die?'" The studies at the Anthropology Research Facility have provided a great deal of information to answer that crucial question.

To get a better understanding of what happens to human bodies after life has ended, the scientists at the Body Farm conduct carefully controlled experiments. Their findings are helping to create an "atlas of decomposition" that is used to solve cases and convict murderers. The subject is not a simple one. Because bodies are subjected to a wide range of conditions in the real world, the experiments at the Body Farm consider many factors. Corpses are left in car trunks, buried in shallow graves, and submerged in water, to name just a few of the variables that have been studied.

> *Determining the precise time that a death took place is extremely important in murder cases because it allows police to better understand what happened and to identify potential suspects. "The crime-scene people find a body in the woods," Bass explained, "and the first thing they want to know is, 'When did he die?'"*

In addition to being rather smelly and generally unpleasant, the process of decomposition is quite complex. Insects play an important role in the events that take place, and Bass and his fellow researchers have analyzed their activity in great detail. In many cases, blowflies will find their way to an exposed corpse in a matter of minutes. They lay eggs, which soon hatch into maggots that feed on the flesh. Though a body undergoing this process the may be a "rotting, maggot-laden mess," to use Bass's own words, it is also loaded with valuable evidence. Because the hatching and growth of maggots follow a predictable timetable, the presence and maturation of the insects allow experts to gauge accurately how much time has passed since the death occurred. The location of maggots on the body can also help investigators determine the cause of death because the insects often mass in an area where the skin has been opened by a wound.

Researchers at the Body Farm have also studied other minute details to aid in criminal investigations. For example, they have analyzed the chemical properties of the residue that is left behind as bodies decompose, documented the effects that fire has on bones, and even classified the precise gases that are emitted by rotting flesh. In addition, the bones of study subjects become part of the school's vast collection of skeletons and are used to train students and to develop powerful new research tools for investigators.

Partly because of the important research carried out at the Body Farm, the University of Tennessee forensic anthropology program has become one of the most respected in the nation. In fact, about one-fourth of the board-certified specialists in that discipline in the United States were educated in Knoxville. In addition, the university operates the National Forensic Academy, which provides specialized training for law enforcement personnel.

The Donation of Bodies

The bodies used by Bass and his colleagues come from two sources. Some are unclaimed corpses contributed by medical examiners. Others are bodies that have been donated for scientific research. As the years have passed, the donations have steadily increased and now make up the majority of the of study subjects, with more than 100 arriving each year to begin their eternal rest at the facility. As Bass has joked, "people these days are just dying to get into the Body Farm."

Not surprisingly, the study of the dead at the Anthropology Research Facility has attracted attention, and not all of it has been positive. Some people feel that it is disrespectful to treat human remains in this way. The biggest controversy erupted in the mid-1990s, when local television news stories announced that some of the unclaimed bodies that ended up at the facility were those of military veterans, many of whom had fallen on hard times and had been homeless prior to dying. This led to the introduction of a bill in the Tennessee legislature that would have banned the use of unclaimed bodies for research at the university. Fortunately for Bass, many of the

Law enforcement officers often attend training sessions at the Body Farm, as in this group shown in the distance through the trees.

state's district attorneys valued the research conducted at the Body Farm. They spoke out against the bill, and it failed to become law.

Bass understands the sensitive nature of the subject and has established guidelines and ceremonies that are intended to uphold the dignity of the deceased individuals whose earthly remains are used at the facility. "We do not mistreat the dead," he has stated. "We have yearly a memorial service which is held here." During this gathering, staff and students pay tribute to the late men and women who aid in the university's studies, and family members of the dead, if known, are invited to attend.

Bass is frequently asked about his own plans for his body after death and whether he will donate his remains to the Body Farm. He plans to leave the decision to his survivors and admits that he has mixed feelings about the subject. "The scientist in me wants to sign the donation papers. But the rest of me can't forget how much I hate flies."

On the Case

As one of the most respected forensic anthropologists in the U.S., Bass takes part in criminal investigations all over the country and has worked on more than 3,000 cases in the course of his career. Often, his help is needed in prosecuting suspected murderers. A Mississippi case that he worked on beginning in 1999 provides a good example of the way his expertise can contribute to a conviction.

In this instance, Bass was called in to help determine when three people—a husband and wife and their four-year-old daughter—had been killed. Due to other factors in the case, this question was crucial to the district attorney's prosecution of the suspected murderer, who was the husband of the girl's grandmother. If it could be shown that the victims were killed on or before December 2, 1993, the case against the suspect would be much stronger. Lacking witnesses or other means to pinpoint the time, the prosecutor asked Bass to review the crime scene photos.

> ———— " ————
>
> *Bass is frequently asked about his own plans for his body after death and whether he will donate his remains to the Body Farm. He admits that he has mixed feelings about the subject. "The scientist in me wants to sign the donation papers. But the rest of me can't forget how much I hate flies."*
>
> ———— " ————

The key clue was found in a close-up photo of one of the victims. In it, Bass spotted several tiny brown objects. They were empty pupa casings—the cocoon-like shelters used by maggots as they metamorphose into flies. This was valuable evidence. When a fly lays an egg on a corpse, it takes two weeks until the newly transformed fly leaves its shelter. Thus, the presence of the empty pupa casings in the photo taken on December 16 scientifically proved that the family members were already dead on December 2. Based on Bass's testimony and other evidence, the suspect was convicted of three counts of first-degree murder. It was thought that he killed his relatives in order to collect a $250,000 life insurance policy he had taken out on his step-granddaughter.

Though not every case he works on proves this conclusive, Bass takes great satisfaction from his efforts to secure justice, especially when they help convict individuals such as the murderer in Mississippi. "If my expertise can help put away even one vicious specimen like that," Bass commented in *Death's Acre*, "then all my years of study and research have been well spent."

In another memorable investigation, Bass looked into the reported death of an American citizen in Mexico in 1998. Madison Rutherford was thought to have perished when his rented truck ran off the freeway and burned. He was insured for $7 million, and the insurance companies asked for Bass's input before paying death benefits to his wife. Upon examining the teeth and bones found in the vehicle, Bass concluded that they belonged not to Rutherford, a 34-year-old white man, but to a 50- or 60-year-old man who was probably of Mexican descent. The evidence suggested that Rutherford had placed someone else's body in the truck and then burned it to fake his own death and collect the insurance money. Almost two years later, Bass's findings were proven true, when Madison Rutherford was found alive and well and living under an assumed identity in Massachusetts. After his arrest, it was revealed that he had stolen a corpse from a cemetery mausoleum and placed it in the vehicle.

Bass has also applied his knowledge to clearing up mysteries from the past. In 1982, he analyzed the remains of the so-called Lindbergh baby—the son of famed aviator Charles Lindbergh—who had been kidnapped and killed in 1932. Bruno Hauptman was convicted of the crime and executed. Bass's analysis found no evidence to refute the idea that Hauptman had carried out the kidnapping. In 2007, Bass examined the exhumed body of early rock-n-roll singer J. P. (the Big Bopper) Richardson, who was killed in a 1959 plane crash along with several other well-known performers. In this instance, Bass's findings disproved several sensational rumors that surrounded the event, including one that held that Richardson had been to shot prior to the crash.

——— *"* ———

Bass feels that forensic television dramas have created interest in his profession, but he feels that they can sometimes be misleading. "On TV, the police solve the case in an hour," he explained. "The investigators already know the answer to everything— or if they do need to ask a question, they make one phone call and get the answer.... It's not that fast and easy in real life."

——— *"* ———

Celebrity Scientist and Author

Though Bass is well known among forensic anthropologists, he has also achieved a certain amount of fame among the general public as well. This began in 1994, when crime novelist Patricia Cornwell published her bestselling fictional book *The Body Farm*, which is partially set at the Anthropology Research Facility. In fact, one of the characters in the book, Dr. Lyall

Death's Acre, *which Bass co-wrote with Jon Jefferson,*
tells stories about his work at the Body Farm.

Shade, is based on Dr. Bass. (Though many people credit Cornwell with creating the "Body Farm" term, it actually predates her book and was coined by an FBI fingerprint expert.) In the years since the novel appeared, Bass and the research facility have frequently been featured in newspaper and magazine articles and in television programs.

In the early 2000s, Bass began working on books of his own. He and his collaborator, Jon Jefferson, have written *Death's Acre* and *Beyond the Body Farm*, which recount some of Bass's professional adventures and major events in his life. The two authors have also produced crime novels that draw on Bass's experiences, publishing them under the pen name Jefferson Bass.

Interest in Bass's work has grown even stronger in recent years due to the popularity of "CSI" and other television dramas that follow the activities of forensic investigators. Bass appreciates the role these programs have played in creating interest in his profession, but he feels that they can sometimes be misleading. "On TV, the police solve the case in an hour," he explained. "The investigators already know the answer to everything—or if they do need to ask a question, they make one phone call and get the answer.... It's not that fast and easy in real life."

Probing the Science of Death

Though he remains involved in activities at the Body Farm, Bass has gradually given up his academic responsibilities over the past 15 years. He retired as a professor in the mid-1990s but remained as the director of the university's forensic anthropology program until 1999. Today, he teaches college courses on occasion and continues to serve on degree committees. "I'm really not retired, I'm just slowly retiring," he told *Tennessee Alumnus Magazine*. In addition, he still consults on forensic cases and is a sought-after public speaker.

Throughout his career, Bass has carried out investigations on dead bodies— work that many people would find too gruesome to endure. Though most of these experiences do not bother him, there are exceptions. "The only forensic cases that give me troubles are the deaths of children," he said, "because here's a life snuffed out early in the game for no reason."

As to the other unfortunate individuals and unpleasant sights he encounters, Bass is able to do his work because he focuses on solving mysteries and is intrigued by the underlying scientific principles that are at play. "I never see a forensic case as death," he said. "You can go out there and that ... individual is dead and in a bad state of repair. But to me, that is a scientific challenge to see if I can figure out who that individual was and what happened to them. And I never see that as death."

Bass also believes that the research he has pioneered sometimes helps others to come to terms with the end of life and that this is part of the reason that the public finds his work so fascinating. "The Body Farm takes what our society often treats as a taboo subject—death—and explores it scientifically," he observed. "We approach death with a combination of objectivity and scientific curiosity, and people seem to find that intriguing, or even comforting. Maybe death isn't so scary after all; maybe it's a natural process, a part of the whole cycle of life."

> "
>
> *"The Body Farm takes what our society often treats as a taboo subject—death—and explores it scientifically," Bass observed. "We approach death with a combination of objectivity and scientific curiosity, and people seem to find that intriguing, or even comforting. Maybe death isn't so scary after all; maybe it's a natural process, a part of the whole cycle of life."*
>
> "

HOME AND FAMILY

Bill Bass and his first wife, Mary Anna Owen, were wed on August 8, 1953. She was an Army dietician at the time and later worked as a nutritionist. The couple had three sons, Charles, William Marvin IV, and James. Mary Anna died of cancer in 1993. Bass married his second wife, Annette Blackbourne, in 1994; she too was diagnosed with cancer, and she passed away in 1996. Two years later, he married Carol Lee Hicks, whom he had known since childhood, and the two continue to reside in Knoxville. In 2002, Bass had his own brush with death when he suffered a serious heart attack, but he has regained his health with the help of a pacemaker.

HOBBIES AND OTHER INTERESTS

Through much of his life, Bass focused most of his attention on his profession. "I never had any hobbies to be honest," he explained. "I worked 60 to 80 hours a week." Though he still maintains a busy schedule, he enjoys going on trips in his recreational vehicle when time allows.

WRITINGS

Nonfiction

Human Osteology: A Laboratory and Field Manual, 1971

The Leavenworth Site Cemetery: Archaeology and Physical Anthropology, 1971
  (with David R. Evans, Richard L. Jantz, and Douglas H. Ubelaker)
Human Evidence in Criminal Justice, 1983 (with Larry Miller and Ramona
  Miller)
*Bodies We've Buried: Inside the National Forensic Academy, the World's Top
  CSI Training School*, 2006 (with Jarrett Hallcox and Amy Welch)

Fiction and Nonfiction, with Jon Jefferson

*Death's Acre: Inside the Legendary Forensic Lab, The Body Farm, Where the
  Dead Do Tell Tales*, 2003 (nonfiction)
Carved in Bone, 2006 (fiction, as Jefferson Bass)
*Beyond the Body Farm: A Legendary Bone Detective Explores Murders, Myster-
  ies, and the Revolution in Forensic Science*, 2007 (nonfiction)
Flesh and Bone, 2007 (fiction, as Jefferson Bass)

HONORS AND AWARDS

Physical Anthropology Award (American Academy of Forensic Sciences):
  1985
National Professor of the Year (Council for the Advancement and Support
  of Education): 1984-1985
Distinguished Fellow (American Academy of Forensic Sciences): 1994

FURTHER READING

Periodicals

Biography, Sep. 2001, p.90
Herald (Glasgow, Scotland), Feb. 17, 2004, p.13
Nashville Tennessean, Jan. 11, 2004
Newsweek, Oct. 23, 2000, p.50
New York Times Magazine, Dec. 3, 2000, p.104
Popular Science, Sep. 1997, p.76

Online Articles

http://news.bbc.co.uk/2/hi/americas/4638835.stm
  (BBC News, "Life on Tennessee's 'Body Farm,'" July 3, 2005)
http://www.harpercollins.com/authors/32695/Dr_Bill_Bass/index.aspx
  (HarperCollins Author, Dr. Bill Bass, "Interviews: Beyond the Body
  Farm," undated)
http://www.hbo.com/autopsy/forensic/the_body_farm.html
  (HBO, Autopsy, "Forensic Features: Pastoral Putrefaction down on the
  Body Farm," undated)

http://www.cbsnews.com/stories/2002/03/13/60II/main503634.shtml
  (60 Minutes, "Dead Men Talking," Aug. 14, 2002)
http://pr.tennessee.edu/alumnus/alumarticle.asp?id=668
  (Tennessee Alumnus Magazine, "Questions from the Grave," Spring
  2006)

ADDRESS

Bill Bass
Department of Anthropology
250 South Stadium Hall
University of Tennessee
Knoxville, TN 37916

WORLD WIDE WEB SITES

http://www.jeffersonbass.com

Sophia Bush 1982-

American Actor
Star of the Hit TV Show "One Tree Hill" and the
Movies *John Tucker Must Die* and *The Hitcher*

BIRTH

Sophia Anna Bush was born on July 8, 1982, in Pasadena,
California, a suburb of Los Angeles. Her father, Charles
William Bush, worked as a photographer, and her mother,
Maureen Bush, was a photography studio manager. Sophia is
their only child.

YOUTH

Growing up in Pasadena, Bush liked to have sleepovers
with her friends. They would stay up watching scary movies

like *Poltergeist*, although no one would be able to sleep afterwards because they would be too frightened.

Bush remembers one of the first people she ever admired was Oprah Winfrey. "When I was a little girl I was obsessed with Oprah.… I just loved her. I loved how powerful she was as a woman.… I think she's amazing!"

EDUCATION

Bush attended Westbridge School for grades seven through 12. The private girls-only school in Los Angeles was small, and there were only 55 girls in her graduating class. Bush flourished in this environment and was a very outgoing and energetic student. "I was a total education geek," she admitted. "I loved school, I loved learning. I loved doing homework." She also enjoyed playing volleyball on her school's team.

"I was a total education geek," Bush admitted. "I loved school, I loved learning. I loved doing homework."

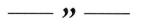

Reading was another one of Bush's favorite activities. She often finished three books in a week, and she took extra English classes to help prepare for college. She was very serious about her studies and spent time as an exchange student in France. After working as a camp counselor, Bush decided she wanted a career working with young children. At first she wanted to become a pediatrician, but later decided she would rather study to become a child psychologist.

Despite growing up so close to Hollywood, Bush never thought of having a career as a performer. She had no desire to be an actor and no interest in the entertainment business. However, her school required all students to participate in a performing arts program, so she had to take part in a play. It was then that she discovered that she loved being onstage, even though it prevented her from playing volleyball. "Part of my school's requirement was to do a play. I was really irritated because I wanted to play volleyball and I had to go and do this play. But there was a moment after the performance when I realized I had gone and been somebody else. I thought, 'If I could do this for the rest of my life, I am set.' It was like love at first sight."

Although acting began as an inconvenient mandatory activity, Bush ended up discovering her dream job. "I decided to follow through with it," she said, "because I never enjoyed anything as much as being up onstage and being someone else." With her parents' support, she decided to pursue a career in acting. "My parents always taught me to believe in myself, and to be true to myself." She went on to act in several plays during high school and began to look for more opportunities to perform.

In 2000, when she was 17 years old, Bush was named the 82nd Rose Queen for the Tournament of Roses in Pasadena. She was chosen from more than 900 other contestants in a selection process that lasted a month. In her yearlong reign as the Rose Queen, Bush appeared at more than 100 community and media functions. Perhaps the most exciting of these was presiding over the Rose Parade and the 2000 Rose Bowl football game.

"Part of my school's requirement was to do a play. I was really irritated because I wanted to play volleyball and I had to go and do this play. But there was a moment after the performance when I realized I had gone and been somebody else. I thought, 'If I could do this for the rest of my life, I am set.' It was like love at first sight."

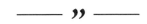

After graduating from high school, Bush enrolled in the University of Southern California in Los Angeles. She was a member of the Kappa Kappa Gamma sorority and served as the social chairperson. She originally studied for a degree in theater, but changed her major to journalism because she wanted to get a better understanding of the public relations side of the acting business.

CAREER HIGHLIGHTS

Bush began auditioning for roles in movies and on television shows while she was still in college. In 2002, she was cast as the girlfriend of the star of *Terminator 3: Rise of the Machines*. But soon after filming began, the director replaced Bush with another actress because she looked too young for the role. She had minor roles in various television shows and movies throughout 2002-2003. Her first major appearance on television was in a three-episode storyline on the drama "Nip/Tuck."

"One Tree Hill"

Bush's big break came in 2003 during her third year of college, when she was 20 years old. She auditioned for a part on a new TV series called "One Tree Hill." After being called back for several auditions and readings, she was offered the role of Brooke Davis, the wild and unpredictable head cheerleader at Tree Hill High. Bush accepted the role, and ten days later she left school in Los Angeles and moved to Wilmington, North Carolina, to begin filming.

The plot of "One Tree Hill" centers on a group of friends who attend high school together in the fictional small town of Tree Hill, North Carolina. Drama unfolds from one episode to the next in ongoing, interconnected stories of friendship, betrayal, romance, heartbreak, rivalry, secrets, lies, deception, and ever-changing alliances among characters. The show started by following the characters through high school but then took a major leap at the start of the 2007-08 season, jumping from the end of high school to the post-college years. "One Tree Hill" became a hit with teen viewers almost immediately and has grown in popularity over the years. Bush was nominated for Teen Choice Awards in 2005 and 2006 for her role as Brooke.

——— " ———

"What I love about [Brooke] is that she's learning lessons on the show that I had to learn, when I was at that age, or in the last few years. Really starting to realize that you've got to make sure that the people you're giving your heart to are treating it with the respect it deserves. And that's a really valuable life lesson, and that's the reason that I love playing her."

——— " ———

Bush's portrayal of Brooke Davis included the character's growth from a fun-loving party girl to a serious fashion designer. Over the course of the first four years of "One Tree Hill," Brooke deals with the demands of school, cheerleading, friendships, romantic relationships, and family problems. In addition to the everyday worries of high school, Brooke also faces many stressful situations not normally encountered by average teens. "What I love about it is that she's learning lessons on the show that I had to learn, when I was at that age, or in the last few years. Really starting to realize that you've got to make sure that the people you're giving your heart to are treating it with the respect it deserves. And that's a really valuable life lesson, and that's the reason that I love playing her."

Some of the "One Tree Hill" drama spilled over into Bush's life off-screen when she became romantically involved with her costar, Chad Michael Murray. The couple met in 2003 on the set of the show and became friends. A romantic relationship soon developed, and they were married in

"One Tree Hill" has been a big hit with teen fans.

2005. However, they separated just a few months later and their marriage ultimately ended in divorce. Bush says of this time in her life, "It devastates me now that I have been reduced to a Hollywood statistic—another joke marriage. I never expected to be married more than once.... But I still be-lieve in love."

After their marriage ended, Bush and Murray were still required to play ro-mantic partners on "One Tree Hill." In 2006, Bush told *CosmoGirl*, "It's not easy for me when the person who Brooke is pining over is someone who I am separating from in real life, and some days are more difficult than oth-ers. But I would never disrespect Brooke as a character, my integrity as an actor, and the fans of the show by not giving her my fullest ability just be-cause of something going on in my personal life. I have to check my per-sonal problems at the door. If anything, this is an exercise for my acting ability!" The experience of having her marriage disintegrate in the media spotlight has made Bush cautious about talking publicly about her love life. By January 2007, Bush was refusing to comment on her divorce, saying only, "That's such a dead horse. We just go to work, and that's it. As for me, I'm happier than I've ever been in my life."

Breaking into Movies

While working on "One Tree Hill," Bush continued to audition for roles in movies. Her first major movie part came in 2005 when she played Zoe in the action film *Supercross*, the story of two brothers who compete in mo-tocross. Although the movie was not a commercial success, it quickly gained a following among fans of motorcycle racing. Then in 2006, she starred in the horror thriller *Stay Alive*. She played October, one of a group of teens who must unravel the mystery behind a series of gruesome real-life deaths that mirror those in a strange new video game. *Stay Alive* be-came a cult hit with teen science fiction fans and video game players alike. Bush enjoyed her role as October, saying, "She's really the mother hen of her group, which is who I have always been. I've always been the mom among all of my buddies and … definitely the girl who can go hang out with the boys and be comfortable."

Bush's first role in a hit movie came in 2006 when she starred in the teen revenge comedy *John Tucker Must Die*. Three high school girls, played by Bush, Ashanti, and Arielle Kebbel, discover they've all been dating the same guy, John Tucker, played by Jesse Metcalfe. Smooth and charming, Tucker seems to be able to get any girl he wants. At first they blame them-selves, but after coming to terms with their discovery they turn their anger toward Tucker. The girls decide to band together to get revenge with the help of a new girl who just transferred to their school, played by Brittany Snow. They give the new student a makeover designed to attract the atten-tion of their target. John Tucker falls for her, and their plot for revenge soon

Bush played Zoe Lang and Steve Howey played KC Carlyle in Supercross.

unfolds. The movie was an instant hit with teens, particularly with teen girls, and Bush won a 2007 Teen Choice Award for her role.

The Hitcher

In 2007 Bush starred in *The Hitcher*, an updated remake of the 1986 film of the same name. The plot of this thriller blends action, horror, and suspense in the frightening story of two college students who decide to pick up a hitchhiker while on a cross-country drive. Bush plays Grace Andrews, part of the unfortunate couple who is being terrorized by "the hitcher." As the story unfolds, Grace must summon the strength to fight off the hitcher's increasingly dangerous attacks. Although the movie was generally panned by critics, it became a hit with teen horror fans. Bush received two Teen Choice Awards in 2007 for her performance as Grace.

The role was Bush's most physically challenging performance, and she did many of her own stunts. Preparing for the stunts required her to be in excellent physical condition, which required a lot of training. "I did about 90 percent of my own stunts.... I started with a trainer and started working really hard back home just to get to a point where my body would be prepared to take the beatings every day and prepared to run through the desert all day on some days and ... dive into and under things and be manhandled and thrown into rooms by large men in the cast.... It was definitely something I had to discipline for and decide to go the extra mile."

> *Filming some of the action scenes in* The Hitcher *was extremely dangerous. "There was one moment where I was in a harness, hanging out the window of a car, going 70 miles per hour down a highway," Bush recalled. "I thought, 'If we get in an accident, I'll be severed in half.'"*

Filming some of the action scenes was extremely dangerous. "There was one moment where I was in a harness, hanging out the window of a car, going 70 miles per hour down a highway," Bush recalled. "I thought, 'If we get in an accident, I'll be severed in half.'" In spite of the danger, she thoroughly enjoyed the role. "I will hold this as the best experience I've ever had. A movie of that scale, with suspense, drama, adrenaline, fear; it is a film that's all across the board for me as an actor."

The success of Bush's performances in "One Tree Hill," *John Tucker Must Die*, and *The Hitcher* has earned her numerous awards. In 2007 she won the most individual Teen Choice Awards, taking home three life-sized surfboard awards in the categories of "Choice Movie Actress-Comedy" (for *John Tucker Must Die*) and "Choice Movie Actress-Horror/Thriller" and "Choice Movie-Breakout Female," both for *The Hitcher*. Bush also won the 2007 Rising Star Award at the Vail Film Festival.

Living With Fame

Starring in a successful TV series and two hit movies has cemented Bush's status as a celebrity. Yet despite all the attention from the media and fans, Bush has said that her life is not that different from what it was before she became a star. "I can go to the mall alone. I can put on a hat and put my hair in a ponytail and go out in jeans and a T-shirt with no makeup on and people almost don't notice me. So life for me is what it used to be, only now I get to do what I love every day. I get to crawl into somebody else's head, and I love that."

John Tucker Must Die *was Bush's first big movie success.*

Bush has preferred to downplay her fame, saying, "I work on a TV show so I'm notable for the TV show, but I'm not a celebrity. I don't call myself a celebrity. I'm an actor." She has been described as a much more thoughtful and smart person than the high school or college students she typically portrays on screen. "People are generally astounded that I'm intelligent or educated or socially conscious or grounded, which is a nice change for me because I'm not a ditzy cheerleader—I wasn't even a cheerleader in high school—I just play one on television."

"The most important thing you have is your relationship with your friends. And it doesn't need to be defined by a clique or defined by your stereotype, it needs to be defined by girls that you love and that you laugh with, and that you get along with."

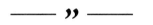

MARRIAGE AND FAMILY

Bush married Chad Michael Murray in April 2005. The marriage lasted just five months, and the couple separated in September 2005. Their divorce was finalized in January 2007.

Bush lives in the house she owns in Wilmington, North Carolina, the town where "One Tree Hill" is filmed. "I love being in North Carolina but it's a struggle being away from home. Even though I'm on this hit show, I still have my best girlfriends who I grew up with and who I went to college with…. The most important thing you have is your relationship with your friends. And it doesn't need to be defined by your stereotype, it needs to be defined by girls that you love and that you laugh with, and that you get along with. And those are the people that are going to be in your life forever."

HOBBIES AND OTHER INTERESTS

Bush enjoys photography, watching movies, spending time with her friends, and playing with her dogs. She has a mastiff, a one-eyed pit bull, and a pomeranian. "I bring my dogs to work every day…. When I have my lunch break and between scenes, I walk them around the lot and play." Reading is still one of her passions. "I was such a bookworm in school and I still am. Everyone on set makes fun of me because I'm always reading, and I still underline things and make notes in the margins."

SELECTED CREDITS

"Nip/Tuck," 2003 (TV series)
"One Tree Hill," 2003- (TV series)
Supercross, 2005 (movie)

Stay Alive, 2006 (movie)
John Tucker Must Die, 2006 (movie)
The Hitcher, 2007 (movie)

HONORS AND AWARDS

Rising Star Award (Vail Film Festival): 2007
Teen Choice Awards: 2007 (three awards), Choice Movie Actress-Comedy, for *John Tucker Must Die*; Choice Movie Actress-Horror/Thriller, for *The Hitcher*; and Choice Movie Breakout-Female, for *The Hitcher*

FURTHER READING

Periodicals

Chicago Sun Times, Jan. 14, 2007, p.D3
CosmoGirl!, Feb. 2006, p.98
Los Angeles Times, Oct. 27, 1999, p.B1
Teen People, Sep. 1, 2005, p.142; Dec. 1, 2005, p.102
USA Today, July 14, 2004, p.D3

Online Articles

http://www.thecinemasource.com/celebrity/interviews/Sophia-Bush-Not-Beating-Around-the-Bush-interview-332-0.html
(TheCinemaSource.com, "Spotlight on Sophia Bush," undated)

http://www.horror.com/php/article-1485-1.html
(Horror.com, "Sophia Bush—Interview with The Hitcher Actor," Dec. 27, 2006)

http://movies.ign.com/articles/721/721026p1.html
(IGN.com, "Interview: Sophia Bush, One of the Stars of *John Tucker Must Die*," July 26, 2006)

http://movies.ign.com/articles/698/698234p1.html
(IGN.com, "Interview: Sophia Bush, 'One Tree Hill' Star Talks *Stay Alive*," Mar. 24, 2006)

http://www.snmag.com/content/view/146/
(Saturday Night Magazine, "Sophia Bush Interview," Jan. 30, 2007)

http://www.ugo.com/channels/filmTv/features/interactivehorror/stayalive_sophia.asp
(UnderGroundOnline, "Sophia Bush of Stay Alive," undated)

ADDRESS

Sophia Bush
The CW Television Network
4000 Warner Boulevard
Burbank, CA 91522

WORLD WIDE WEB SITES

http://www.cwtv.com/shows/one-tree-hill
http://www.myspace.com/johntucker
http://www.neverpickupstrangers.com

Zac Efron 1987-

American Actor and Singer
Star of the Disney TV Movies *High School Musical*
and *High School Musical 2* and the Feature Film
Hairspray

BIRTH

Zachary David Alexander Efron was born on October 18,
1987, in San Luis Obispo, California. He is the son of David
Efron, an engineer at a power plant, and Starla Efron, a secre-
tary at the same plant. Efron has one younger brother, Dylan.

YOUTH AND EDUCATION

Efron grew up in Arroyo Grande, a suburban town north of Los Angeles on the Pacific Coast. "I grew up in California completely ignorant of the entertainment industry," he said. "I grew up as a regular guy with a regular life. I went to school and got good grades. I have the most normal family in the world."

One of his parents was always at home when Efron got home from school, and they always made sure he did his homework. "My parents were very strict," he said. If he play-wrestled too roughly with his little brother, which he often did, he was grounded. Once he was grounded for a week after he cut his hair and then lied about it.

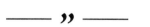

> "I grew up in California completely ignorant of the entertainment industry," Efron said. "I grew up as a regular guy with a regular life. I went to school and got good grades. I have the most normal family in the world."

Mostly, Efron recalls a happy childhood in which he often burst into song or dance. "When Zac was a toddler, after watching *The Wizard of Oz*, we found him emulating the Tin Man dance," his father told *Rolling Stone*. "Over time we noticed that he had an uncanny ability to listen to a song on the radio, memorize the lyrics, and sing it back a capella with the correct rhythm and pitch."

In elementary school, Efron liked playing sports, especially baseball. But he was small and didn't play that well. Meanwhile, his musical talents were blossoming. When he was 11 years old, he told his parents that he didn't want to play baseball anymore. They suggested that he take piano lessons. Reluctant at first, Efron eventually agreed. He began taking lessons with Jeremy Mann, who also worked for a company that staged musicals. Efron's upbeat personality charmed Mann immediately. "The first time I met him," Mann remarked, "I said to myself, 'This kid's going to grow up to be Brad Pitt.' He's probably the most charismatic little kid I've ever met."

Becoming an Actor

Mann thought Efron would be a natural performer. He encouraged the 11-year-old to audition for *Gypsy*, which was being staged by the Pacific Conservatory of the Performing Arts. Efron needed a big push from his father to show up for the tryouts. "I went into this audition kicking and scream-

*Efron appearing on "The Suite Life of Zack and Cody"
with Brenda Song (left) and Ashley Tisdale (right).*

ing, and little did I know my dad had just showed me the coolest thing on earth," he said. He got a small part as a newsboy and appeared in more than 70 performances of *Gypsy*. "From day one, I got addicted to being on stage and getting the applause and laughter," he said.

After *Gypsy*, Efron said, "[I] started auditioning for every single play that was in our area. Luckily, I booked some of the roles and started doing very well." His favorite role was as Wendy's brother John in *Peter Pan*. "That was a really fun part because I got to fly around on a 'fly' wire," he said. "I was hovering over people in the audience. I actually knocked off a guy's toupee once." A lot of the fun came from the friendships he made with other young actors. Many of them appeared in the same plays, and they liked to hang out together backstage.

In middle school, Efron took drama classes to learn more about his craft and be with students who shared his passion for performing. When he was 14, his drama teacher recognized his talent and arranged an audition for him. His mother drove him three hours to Los Angeles, where his successful reading landed him an agent.

For the next few months, mother and son repeated the trek to Los Angeles. Efron auditioned for television and film roles, but was repeatedly rejected. Tired of the long commute, his mother told him that unless he got some jobs within the next year, she was through being the chauffeur. Before her deadline, Efron landed a few small television roles and commercials. In 2003 he appeared in the TV drama "E.R.," playing a young teenager who got caught in gang crossfire and died on the operating table. After that, he landed TV guest spots more regularly. A big break came in 2004, when he co-starred in the made-for-TV movie *Miracle Run* as a developmentally disabled teenager. The movie, including Efron's performance, was well received.

Between acting jobs, Efron attended his hometown high school and worked hard to keep up his grades. English was his favorite subject, and chemistry was his least favorite, although he got straight A's in the class. Acting jobs kept him too busy to play sports or participate in after-school clubs or high-school theater. Eventually, Efron found it hard to keep up with his classes, and he left school in the middle of 10th grade. "I enrolled in junior college courses—that's how I graduated," he said.

CAREER HIGHLIGHTS

Efron's first consistent acting job came in 2004. It started with "Summerland," a TV series about a career woman, played by Lori Loughlin, who was left to raise her sister's three children after a fatal car crash. Efron appeared as Cameron Bale, a 14-year-old neighbor who became involved with one of the children, played by Kay Panabaker. His performance impressed the producers so much that he was hired to be a regular member of the cast. "I really got to see what acting was like," he said of his "Summerland" experience. "It was a big break in the business." Unfortunately, "Summerland" was cancelled after a single season. Efron was disappointed at the time, but his career was about to skyrocket.

High School Musical

In 2005 the Disney Channel began casting for an original film about teenagers who get together to put on a musical in their high school. *High School Musical* begins as two teens on vacation at a ski resort are forced to sing karaoke together at a New Year's Eve party. Athletic Troy Bolton (played by Zac Efron) and brainy Gabriella Montez (played by Hudgens) enjoy their duet, although neither has done much singing before. When Gabriella transfers to Troy's high school, the two of them end up in their own cliques. They think about trying out for the school musical, although their friends disapprove and their musical rivals, twins Sharpay and Ryan, scheme to stop them. Troy and Gabriella have to withstand the disapproval of their

Efron in scenes from High School Musical *and* High School Musical 2.

friends to be together, a theme that the creators of the movie acknowledge is reminiscent of the Broadway musicals *West Side Story* and *Grease*.

Efron was one of many teenage actors to audition for the film, and the competition was fierce. He had to go through several rounds of tryouts. "They would send you to these rooms to learn the songs and the dances," he said. "Then you would rehearse. You would audition and then all you would hear was, 'OK, we'll call you.' It was nerve wracking. I mean, you never know what's going on in a director's head."

Efron's background in local musical theater productions gave him an edge and the stamina to make it through the marathon auditions. "I had it easier than some of the guys.... Some of them were passing out!" he said. "It was Broadway-style, seven-and-a-half hours of singing, acting, and dancing. And then we had to play basketball. I was probably weakest at that."

> "I went into this audition kicking and screaming, and little did I know my dad had just showed me the coolest thing on earth," he said. "From day one, I got addicted to being on stage and getting the applause and laughter."

Some of the male and female aspirants were asked to audition together. Efron was asked to sing with Vanessa Anne Hudgens, who was trying out for the role of Gabriella. "It was fun; we were put together from the beginning," he said. "And to some degree, I think that helped us out because we really got to know each other." At the end of the tryouts, it was Efron, along with Hudgens, who landed the starring roles. Efron called Troy a "dream character to play. He's kind of like Danny Zuko in *Grease* [played by John Travolta in the movie version of the musical]. I think that every guy would like being more like Troy when they were in high school. I wish I was more like him because he's so good. He's so good at basketball."

It took just six weeks to make *High School Musical*. For the first two weeks the cast was put through day-long rehearsals at the southwest Utah film site. After Efron went over the singing and dancing routines, he went to basketball practice with his fellow *Musical* teammates. Then came four weeks of filming. Despite the hectic schedule, the young actors enjoyed being with each other during the production. "The whole cast would hang out after every day of shooting," Efron said. "We'd go and eat dinner and we just did fun stuff together and it made being on the set a lot more fun."

High School Musical Becomes a Hit

High School Musical proved to be a blockbuster for Disney. The January 2006 television premiere averaged almost 7.7 million viewers, and repeat telecasts drew many millions more. The show won an Emmy for Outstanding Children's Program as well as a 2006 Teen Choice Award for Choice Comedy/Musical Program. Disney has aired several different versions of the musical, including a sing-along version with song lyrics; a dance-along version, in which cast members show the audience footwork routines; and a pop-up version, which includes information about the making of the movie. It also produced nationwide concert tours and even ice shows.

The soundtrack of the movie was in the Top 10 on the Billboard charts for over five months and became the biggest selling CD of 2006, with more than four million in sales. For Efron, the music in *High School Musical* is a bit of an embarrassment. "I didn't sing on the first album," he admitted. "It wasn't my voice in the movie. Even though I wanted to do it." The DVD, which included the original and sing-along versions, broke sales records in 2006 when 1.2 million copies were sold in its first six days, making it the fastest-selling TV movie of all time.

> ———— **"** ————
>
> *"The whole cast would hang out after every day of shooting," Efron said about making* **High School Musical.** *"We'd go and eat dinner and we just did fun stuff together and it made being on the set a lot more fun."*
>
> ———— **"** ————

After the success of *High School Musical,* producers of an earlier Efron movie moved to capitalize on his fame. Efron had filmed *The Derby Stallion* before *High School Musical,* but it wasn't released right away; instead, it went straight to DVD in 2007. *Stallion* is the story of a conflicted 15-year-old boy (played by Efron) who hooks up with an elderly horseman and ends up training for the Derby Cup. Efron spent weeks learning how to ride a horse in order to play the part. Beth Johnson of *Entertainment Weekly* wrote that although the film is "full of cliches," the "relationship between boy and mentor is touching, Efron is adorable, family values are applauded and, well, you have the satisfaction of knowing how it will all turn out."

Hairspray

In the winter of 2007, the cast of *High School Musical* began a 40-city concert tour without Efron, who was busy filming the big-screen musical

Link Larkin (Efron) and Tracy Turnblad (Nikki Blonsky)
share a moment in Hairspray.

Hairspray. The movie tells the story of Tracy Turnblad (played by Nikki Blonsky), a bubbly, overweight Baltimore teenager who longs to sing and dance on a local TV show. Efron landed the role of slick-haired Link Larkin, the heartthrob of the dance show and Tracy's love interest. John Travolta, dressed in drag, plays Tracy's mother.

Efron almost blew his initial audition for Link. "I saw this sweet, goofy kid," Adam Shankman, the director and choreographer of *Hairspray,* told *USA Today.* "I thought he was too light. Link is more cool. Then my sister, Jennifer, one of the executive producers, said to me, 'You passed on him? Are you out of your mind? He's the biggest star on the planet to anyone under 15.'" Shankman called Efron back, gave him more specific directions about Link's character, and was impressed enough by Efron's second audition to hire him. Nikki Blonsky thought Efron nailed the part. "He just jumps off the screen and right into every girl's heart," she said.

For Efron, working in a major Hollywood production was a dream come true. "I sat down to a table read, and I was next to Michelle Pfeiffer, and on the other side of me was Amanda Bynes and across from me were John Travolta and Chris Walken," he said. "It was such a star-studded cast, I couldn't believe I was sharing a table—let alone working in the same movie as them." Sharing the screen with Travolta was a special thrill for Efron, who has idolized the actor since seeing him in the 1978 movie *Grease.* "I remember thinking musicals were cool all because of John," he said.

> **"**
>
> *According to Adam Shankman, the director of* Hairspray, *Efron almost blew his initial audition for Link. "I saw this sweet, goofy kid," Shankman said. "I thought he was too light. Link is more cool. Then my sister, Jennifer, one of the executive producers, said to me, 'You passed on him? Are you out of your mind? He's the biggest star on the planet to anyone under 15.'"*
>
> **"**

Hairspray was filmed in Toronto, Canada, which marked the first time Efron had ever lived on his own. "Toronto was where I grew up, and it happened quick," he said. "I was self-sufficient in a matter of weeks. It was great, but then I started clinging to the people I was working with. I would come to the set and just observe, even if I wasn't working that day."

Hairspray opened in July 2007 to mostly good reviews. Susan Wloszczyna of *USA Today* noted that the part of Link Larkin allowed Efron to escape from the "squeaky-clean confines" of *High School Musical*. "He lets loose with a lusty yelp during a solo number, 'Ladies Choice,' which finally showcases his inviting baritone in all its unadulterated glory," Wloszczyna wrote.

High School Musical 2

Soon after he finished work on *Hairspray*, Efron reunited with the original *High School Musical* cast and the director, Kenny Ortega, to film the movie's sequel. *High School Musical 2* focuses on a scheme by Sharpay to woo Troy away from Gabriella. School has let out for summer vacation, leading up to senior year. The East High classmates all have summer jobs at a country club controlled by Sharpay's wealthy family. But things become tense as Sharpay schemes to break up Gabriella and Troy. Troy must decide whether to pursue the advantages that are available from Sharpay's wealthy family—even if it means neglecting Gabriella and his friends. It's a difficult summer, but all is resolved as the group participates in the country club's annual talent show, an opportunity for more great song-and-dance numbers from the cast.

> ——— " ———
>
> *According to Efron,* **High School Musical 2** *offered new insight into his character. "Troy is balancing a lot of temptations," he said. "He's very goal-oriented, almost to a fault. It was fun to play the other side of him. He gets lured to the dark side."*
>
> ——— " ———

According to Efron, *High School Musical 2* offered new insight into his character. "Troy is balancing a lot of temptations," he said. "He's very goal-oriented, almost to a fault. It was fun to play the other side of him. He gets lured to the dark side."

High School Musical 2 was eagerly anticipated by the first movie's many fans. More than 17 million people watched its premiere on the Disney Channel on August 17, 2007, making the sequel the most watched basic cable telecast in history. The movie generated mostly positive reviews. Robert Bianco of *USA Today* called the sequel "a first-rate family film: sweet, smart, bursting with talent and energy, and awash in innocence." At the 2007 Teen Choice Awards, *High School Musical 2* won the award for Choice TV Movie, and Efron won the award for Choice Male Hottie. Efron sang all of his character's songs in the sequel, although he acknowledged that none of the actors have control over the finished product. "Once it's edited, the people in this cast sound like Mariah Carey," he said. "There's skill involved [but] with computers these days, you never know."

The dancing and singing scenes are part of what makes
High School Musical 2 *so much fun.*

Future Plans

As one of the hottest young actors in Hollywood, Efron is sifting through many offers. Currently, he has two film projects in development. One is tentatively called *Seventeen*, which has been described as a reverse of the 1988 Tom Hanks film *Big*. Instead of a kid turning into an adult overnight, it's about an adult who turns into a kid. Efron described his starring character as a man who "wishes he could go back to high school again, and sure enough, he wakes up and he is young again, he is 17 again." Another project in development is a new musical version of the 1984 movie *Footloose*, which originally starred Kevin Bacon. Efron would star in the new film, which would be directed and choreographed by Kenny Ortega.

Then there's the *High School Musical* franchise, which is slated to go from TV to a big-screen production. "I would love to do a third *High School Musical* ... to finish off on the silver screen would be a great legacy for the *High School Musical* series to leave," Efron said.

HOME AND FAMILY

Efron lives in an apartment in North Hollywood, but he often visits his parents and younger brother in Arroyo Grande. When in Los Angeles, he likes to hang out with his childhood friends who live in the area. "These are the friends I used to do theater with," he said. Staying close to old friends helps Efron keep his teen-idol stardom in perspective. "I could show you 500 kids in L.A. who are my height, weight, hair color, and age," he said. "We're a dime a dozen. Why did I get the parts I did? Who knows? But the minute I start thinking it's because I was special, that's when I know I'm in trouble."

Efron has been linked romantically to his *High School Musical* co-star Vanessa Anne Hudgens. While calling her an "amazing girl," Efron has downplayed their relationship and expressed frustration at the paparazzi—photographers who snap celebrity pictures for sale—who are always pointing cameras in their faces when they go out. "I never in a million years saw myself as dealing with the paparazzi," he said. "It seems it wouldn't be that big of an issue, but there are personal things you don't want captured on camera."

SELECTED CREDITS

Miracle Run, 2004 (TV movie)
"Summerland," 2004 - 05 (TV series)
High School Musical, 2006 (TV movie)
The Derby Stallion, 2007 (movie released on DVD)
Hairspray, 2007 (movie)
High School Musical 2, 2007 (TV movie)

HONORS AND AWARDS

Teen Choice Award: 2006 (two awards), TV-Choice Breakout Star and
 Choice Chemistry for *High School Musical* (with Vanessa Hudgens);
 2007, Choice Male Hottie
Hollywood Film Award: 2007, Ensemble Acting (with the cast of *Hairspray*)

FURTHER READING
Books

Norwich, Grace. *Zac Attack: An Unauthorized Biography*, 2006 (juvenile)

Periodicals

Chicago Sun Times, Aug. 19, 2007, p.D2
Entertainment Weekly, Aug. 31, 2007, p.34
Los Angeles Times, Aug. 27, 2007, p.E1
New York Times, Mar. 11, 2007, Arts and Leisure section, p.1
People, Sep. 3, 2007, p.62

Rolling Stone, Aug. 23, 2007, p.38
Time, Aug. 27, 2007, p.9
USA Today, July 20, 2007, p.D1

Online Articles

http://www.movieweb.com/dvd/news/56/12756.php
(Movieweb.com, "Zac Efron and Vanessa Anne Hudgens Sing Their
Praises for *High School Musical*," May 22, 2006)
http://pbskids.org/itsmylife/celebs/interviews/zac.html
(PBSKids.org, "Zac Efron," undated)
http://sanluisobispo.com/ticket/story/95872.html
(SanLuisObispo.com, "A Rising Star," July 19, 2007)
http://content.scholastic.com/browse/article.jsp?id=3747512
&FullBreadCrumb=%3Ca+href%3D%22
(Scholastic, "Zac Efron Talks Troy," Aug. 22, 2007)
http://www.timeforkids.com/TFK/kidscoops/story/0,14989,1169108,00.html
(Time for Kids, "The Scoop on High School Musical," Mar. 2, 2006)
http://www.thestar.com/entertainment/article/242589
(Toronto Star, "Zac Efron: The High School Hunk," Aug. 4, 2007)
http://www.usatoday.com/life/television/reviews/2007-08-16-hsm2_n.htm
(USAToday, "*High School Musical* Sequel Holds onto Note of Inno-
cence," Aug. 16, 2007)

ADDRESS

Zac Efron
Disney Channel
3800 West Alameda Avenue
Burbank, CA 91505

WORLD WIDE WEB SITES

http://tv.disney.go.com/disneychannel/originalmovies/highschoolmusical
/index.html

Bindi Irwin 1998-

Australian Wildlife Enthusiast
Host of the TV Series "Bindi the Jungle Girl" and
"Planet's Best with Terri and Bindi"

BIRTH

Bindi Sue Irwin was born on July 24, 1998, in Queensland, Australia. Her father, Steve Irwin, was an Australian-born animal expert. He was best known for his television program, "The Crocodile Hunter," an internationally broadcast wildlife documentary series. Steve Irwin co-hosted the program with Bindi's mother, Terri Raines Irwin, an American-born conservationist. The couple owned and operated the Australia Zoo, a giant wildlife park. Terri Irwin has continued to run the zoo since Steve Irwin's death in 2005. Bindi has a younger brother, Robert.

Bindi's name means "young girl" in the language spoken by Aborigines, the indigenous people of Australia. Steve Irwin once named a female crocodile "Bindi" that he caught in Aboriginal territory. He moved the crocodile to the zoo for its protection. Years later, when his daughter was born, "he saw how tiny and sweet and special she was," Terri Irwin recalled, "and [he] said, 'I have to name her Bindi after my favorite crocodile.'" Bindi's middle name, Sue, was also inspired by an animal—her father's pet dog, Suey.

EARLY CHILDHOOD

Bindi has been around cameras since her birth. Determined not to be absentee parents, Steve and Terri Irwin made a point of bringing Bindi along on their many field trips for "The Crocodile Hunter" and other wildlife projects. Six days after she was born, the Irwins took Bindi to Fraser Island, off the coast of Australia, where they were filming a documentary about wildlife. By the time she was a year old, Bindi had made 110 airplane trips, including 10 visits to the United States. "It's exciting doing things with Bindi because you can experience things through a child's eyes," Terri Irwin said.

> "She is remarkably gifted with animals," Terri Irwin said when Bindi was only two years old. "Her dad's got the gift and she's got the same gift—whether it's koalas, camels, or crocodiles."

Steve Irwin was famous for capturing crocodiles and many other endangered species in order to save them from poachers (people who illegally kill wildlife for profit). "My daughter is going to grow up doing this," Irwin said, when Bindi was just a toddler. "There's this shot of me with Bindi and a big croc, and he's all teeth.... She's like 'Oooh!' It's sure to make some mothers cringe." In fact, several years later, Steve Irwin was criticized in the media for holding Bindi's little brother, Robert, too close to a crocodile. But Irwin insisted that he only brought his children into controlled situations and would never put them in danger.

Irwin brought many of the animals he captured to the Australian Zoo. As directors of the zoo, Steve and Terri Irwin tried to duplicate the animals'

Bindi at age four with her parents, Terri and Steve Irwin.

natural habitats as much as possible, without the use of cages or pens. Visitors to the zoo can mingle with koala bears, feed the kangaroos, and pet the non-poisonous snakes. Bindi has grown up surrounded by the zoo's wildlife, which became her earliest playmates. "She is remarkably gifted with animals," Terri Irwin said when Bindi was only two years old. "Her dad's got the gift and she's got the same gift—whether it's koalas, camels, or crocodiles."

One of Bindi's first pets was a small carpet python, which she liked to cuddle and kiss. One day the snake bit her nose. "She just looked very surprised," her mother recalled. "Then she kissed it again and it bit her lip. She learned a valuable lesson, that some snakes bite." To Bindi's parents, learning to handle animals with respect was very important. Her father often told her "to treat animals as you would like to be treated."

When Bindi was three years old, her father built her a two-story treehouse. As Bindi has grown, she has spent more and more time there. "I love it in my treehouse," she said. "It's the best place to be, pretty much. I just go there to sleep over sometimes. My little brother comes to visit me for a little sleepover as well." Many of Bindi's pets spend time with her in the treehouse, too. "I have Blackie, my black-headed python," Bindi said. "I also have Cornie the snake. He sleeps with me at night. I also have Jaffa, my koala (bear), and Ocker, my favorite cockatoo. And I have other birds that stay with me. And Candy, my pet rat, sometimes stays with me."

EDUCATION

Bindi is home-schooled by a teacher on the zoo grounds. When she is traveling for wildlife filming, the teacher accompanies her. Her favorite subject is creative writing. By the time she was six, she was writing a journal of her adventures called "Bindi's Say," which her father posted on his web site.

In addition to her schoolwork, Bindi has daily chores when she's at home on the zoo grounds. She checks on many of the animals, including the shingle-back skinks, the large lizards that are among her favorite animals at the zoo. To make sure all the skinks are accounted for in their enclosure, she digs up sand, lifts rocks, and moves small logs.

CAREER HIGHLIGHTS

By the time she was seven, Bindi was no longer just watching her father interact with animals during his film shoots—she was often an active participant. She was such a natural presence on camera, and so fearless around the wildlife, that her parents decided that she ought to have a television series of her own. Steve Irwin negotiated a deal with the Discovery Channel for a show, and filming for "Bindi the Jungle Girl" began in 2005.

The premise of the series is to show children how animals live around the world and describe the efforts of wildlife lovers to protect them. "I get to grow up with animals," Bindi said. "I can teach people. I'm not an actor, I'm a teacher. I can teach people about animals."

The Death of Steve Irwin

Before "Jungle Girl" ever aired, however, Bindi's father was killed. On September 4, 2005, Steve Irwin and a cameraman were filming dangerous sea creatures in the waters off Queensland, Australia. A 220-pound stingray suddenly became defensive and thrust the 8-inch poisonous barb on its tail upward, striking Irwin in the heart. Irwin pulled the barb out, but the damage was too great, and he soon died.

At the time of the accident, Bindi was in Tasmania, the island-state off Australia, with her mother and brother. Devastated by her father's death, Bindi nonetheless found the courage to speak at his funeral. "My daddy was my hero," she said. "He was always there for me when I needed him. He listened to me and taught me to do many things. But most of all he was fun. I know that daddy had an important job. He was working to change the world so that everyone would love wildlife like he did.... I don't want daddy's passion to ever end. I want to help endangered wildlife just like he did."

Deciding to Continue with "Jungle Girl"

Bindi, like her mother, believed the death of her father was a freak accident and the animal was not to blame. But the question of whether to continue filming "Jungle Girl" remained. Terri Irwin said that she discussed it with Bindi before coming to a decision. "Grief is a road every individual travels in their own way," she told the *Times* of London. "Bindi said that she wanted to get back to filming right away. We wanted to get right back out there and stand proud."

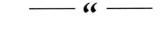

"My daddy was my hero," Bindi said. "He was always there for me when I needed him. He listened to me and taught me to do many things. But most of all he was fun."

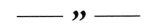

Over the next year, preparation for Bindi's show continued. A two-level treehouse, based on the treehouse built by her father, was assembled as the main "Jungle Girl" set. It features tree branches and bushes, along with a bedroom, a long wooden table with a computer, bean bag chairs, and a play area. "All of her animal friends, from iguana and snakes and wombats—everything comes to visit her," her mother said.

"Bindi the Jungle Girl" debuted on the Discovery Kids cable channel in July 2007. A good deal of the program is devoted to film of animals in the wild, including whales, elephants, lions, tigers, orangutans, big birds like macaws, and small lizards like the gecko. Steve Irwin is featured in early episodes, filmed prior to his death, doing things like helping an injured lion and climbing trees to visit the nests of endangered orangutans. Continuing the family tradition, Bindi and her mother also travel around the globe to show viewers wildlife in its natural habitat. In those settings, Bindi says she always follows her father's words of caution: "if it's out in the wilderness, like snakes, leave it alone, and just look at it. Don't touch it."

Bindi also narrates many stories close to home, such as animal dental care at the Australia Zoo. "I'm trying to get across the message that 'don't be

Bindi with the Crocmen, the backup band for her Discovery Kids TV show.

afraid of animals,'" she said. "Some people think that I would be afraid of them, but I'm never ever afraid of an animal. I just get excited."

In each "Jungle Girl" episode, Bindi sings and dances to animal-themed songs with the show's backup band, called the Crocmen. Another program feature is "Bindi's Video Blog," in which she answers email questions sent to her at discovery.com. Bindi works hard on "Jungle Girl," but she does not mind the effort. "I love it!" she said about her TV show. "Animals are my friends, and this means I get to be with all my friends."

In his enthusiastic review in the *Chicago Sun Times*, Doug Elfman wrote, "'Jungle Girl' moves fast, as you'd expect of a kid's show, but it's smooth, sleek, stylish, and mesmerizing. Like 'The Crocodile Hunter,' it's environmentally conscious education completely disguised as amazing, upbeat entertainment."

Other Projects

Bindi hosted a television special called "My Daddy the Crocodile Hunter," which aired in June 2007 on the Animal Planet cable channel. The program featured family video clips of Steve Irwin and his family interacting with animals and teaching Bindi and her brother how to care for wildlife habitats. There was also film of Bindi assisting her father on his last crocodile research adventure in August 2006.

Also in June 2007, Animal Planet began featuring Bindi and her mother as co-hosts of "Planet's Best with Bindi and Terri." On this Sunday evening program, the Irwins introduce documentaries and specials about wildlife and the people who work with them. The films, which come from Animal Planet's extensive library of previously seen shows, span the globe. Bindi and her mother discuss the films from their home at the Australia Zoo. They also give viewers a glimpse of the many animals on the zoo property and answer questions people send in about wildlife issues.

In August 2007 Bindi introduced a new children's clothing line called Bindi Wear International, which is sold online at the Australia Zoo web site. All profits from the clothing go to support the zoo's conservation programs. "My daddy was working to change the world so everyone would love wildlife like he did," Bindi said. "Now it's our turn to help." The clothing line is designed by Pamela DiStasi, an Irwin family friend. The clothes feature animal prints and themes and include messages about wildlife and environmental conservation written in Bindi's handwriting.

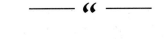

According to reviewer Doug Elfman, "'Jungle Girl' moves fast, as you'd expect of a kid's show, but it's smooth, sleek, stylish and mesmerizing. Like 'The Crocodile Hunter,' it's environmentally conscious education completely disguised as amazing, upbeat entertainment."

In addition to appearing on TV, Bindi has also appeared with her backup band, the Crocmen, in a live stage show. The first performances were staged in 2007 in Australia and the United States. Bindi sang and danced in the show, which had an animal theme. "I just like the feeling of all the people actually cheering for me and saying, 'Bindi, Bindi.' ... I just feel like I've got a place there," she said. "It feels really good when I get on stage." The shows have included appearances by her mother, who brings animals on stage to show the audiences, and by the Australian musical groups the Wiggles and the Qantas Choir.

Bindi's stage shows in the United States were scheduled around speaking appearances that she did on behalf of the Australian tourism board, to attract American visitors to Australia. She also spoke as an advocate of wildlife preservation. The youngest person ever to speak to the National Press Club in Washington DC, Bindi told the assembled reporters, "It is very sad that in my lifetime a lot of wildlife could disappear. We could lose tigers and gorillas and even my favorite koalas. We need to help my daddy's work and make this world a perfect place for animals."

Is It Too Much?

The adults who help guide Bindi's career have faced criticism that she is working too hard and that she is being denied a normal childhood. According-

"It is very sad that in my lifetime a lot of wildlife could disappear. We could lose tigers and gorillas and even my favorite koalas. We need to help my daddy's work and make this world a perfect place for animals."

ing to Catherine Dawson March, a columnist for the Canadian newspaper the *Globe and Mail,* "Bindi Irwin, the nine-year-old daughter of crocodile hunter Steve Irwin, seems a little too 'on' for her age, a little too ebullient, and isn't it a little early to be hosting your own wildlife series when your dad's been dead only a year?" Other critics have speculated that Bindi has been pushed into several projects at once as a way to continue Steve Irwin's money-making wildlife activities. John Stainton, the family's career manager, dismisses the criticism as unfounded, saying that she has been eager to spread her father's conservation message. "I think they (critics) don't understand that this little girl is very much enjoying what she is doing. She is in control," Stainton told the *Gold Coast Bulletin.*

Terri Irwin has also weighed in on this issue, telling the *Times* of London, "I think Bindi's schedule is a lot easier than a lot of children's. There's a lot of kids who have soccer practices, dance lessons, and parents start feeling like a chauffeur and kids start to feel overwhelmed. Bindi is certainly not like that."

For her part, Bindi insists that she enjoys working with animals and traveling with her mother and brother to different parts of the world. "I just love this life so much!" she said. "I couldn't stand it if I was in an apartment with a goldfish!"

When asked what she wants do when she grows up, Bindi didn't hesitate. "Exactly what I am doing now," she said. "I want to be what my dad was. I want to do wildlife stuff, pretty much."

HOME AND FAMILY

Bindi lives with her mother and brother, Robert, in a house on the grounds of the Australia Zoo, a neighborhood that Bindi loves. "Every morning I wake up to elephants screeching and tigers chuffing—they don't roar, they chuff," she said. "As soon as you walk outside the front door, you've got the whole zoo, which is very nice." Bindi and Robert watch a video of their father every day while they eat breakfast. "We've got so much terrific footage of Steve, that he'll be part of our conservation work forever," Terri Irwin said. "And it's great to know, for kids particularly, that when your hero dies, everything he stood for lives on." During her spare time, Bindi takes piano lessons and martial arts lessons, and she is also learning how to surf.

SELECTED CREDITS

Bindi Kidfitness, 2006 (DVD)
"Bindi the Jungle Girl," 2007- present (TV series)
"Animal Planet's Best with Bindi and Terri," 2007- present (TV series)
"My Daddy the Crocodile Hunter," 2007 (TV special)

FURTHER READING

Periodicals

Chicago Sun Times, June 6, 2007, p.43
Daily Telegraph (Australia), Sep. 9, 2000, p. 120; Sep. 21, 2006, p.2; July 18, 2007, p.6
Globe and Mail (Toronto), Sep. 28, 2007, p.R39
Gold Coast Bulletin (Australia), Sep. 12, 2002; Oct. 17, 2006, p.3
New York Post, Sep. 5, 2006, p.2
People, Oct. 16, 2000, p.93; Oct. 30, 2006, p.72; June 18, 2007, p.133
Pretoria News (South Africa), July 4, 2007, p.6
Times (London), Jan. 20, 2007, p.50
Women's Wear Daily, Aug. 14, 2007, p.14

ADDRESS

Bindi Irwin
Discovery Kids
7700 Wisconsin Avenue
Bethesda, MD 20814

WORLD WIDE WEB SITES

http://www.australiazoo.com
http://kids.discovery.com/tv/bindi
http://animal.discovery.com/tv/planets-best/planets-best.html
http://www.crocodilehunter.com.au/crocodile_hunter/about_steve_terri/
bindi_say.html

Lisa Ling 1973-

American Journalist
Host of the National Geographic Television Show
"Explorer"

BIRTH

Lisa Ling was born on August 30, 1973, in Sacramento, California. Her parents are Douglas Ling, an aviation administrator, and Mary Ling, the owner of an import-export company. Both of her parents are of Chinese descent. She has one younger sister, Laura.

YOUTH AND EDUCATION

Ling was raised near the McClellan Air Force Base outside of Sacramento, where her father worked. Her parents divorced when she was seven years old. Ling and her younger sister lived with their father, but their mother was a constant, reassuring presence as the two siblings went through childhood and adolescence. "Even though I didn't grow up with her, she was a very integral part of my life," said Ling.

> *"People would get in my face and call me Risa Ring, Ching Chong, Lisa Yellow. There were a lot of really evil kids in high school," Ling recalled. "As a kid I was embarrassed to be Asian because I didn't look like everyone else. I wasn't an outcast, but I didn't like being different."*

Ling was a good student, and she participated in debate and other extracurricular activities at school. She was one of only a handful of Asian-American students in school, however, and at times she endured racial taunts from classmates. "People would get in my face and call me Risa Ring, Ching Chong, Lisa Yellow," she recalled. "There were a lot of really evil kids in high school." Ling admitted that this ugly behavior took a toll on her self-image. "As a kid I was embarrassed to be Asian because I didn't look like everyone else. I wasn't an outcast, but I didn't like being different."

Ling graduated from high school in 1990. Two years later, in 1992, she enrolled at the University of Southern California (USC) in Los Angeles. She studied history at USC and even made the dean's list as a freshman. But Ling left college before graduating because she decided to devote all her attention to her television career—a career that began back when she was in high school.

CAREER HIGHLIGHTS

Ling's rise to television stardom began at age 16, when she was still in high school. Her speech class teacher (who was also her debate team coach) announced that a new local television show targeted at teens was holding auditions at a nearby mall. Ling went to the mall after school and videotaped a short audition. Soon after, she was stunned to learn that the show's producers wanted to talk to her about serving as one of the show's four teen hosts. After a quick flurry of meetings, Ling found herself appearing on TV every week as a host of "Scratch," a teen magazine program that was syndicated to stations around the country. She co-hosted the show from 1989 to 1991.

The demands of Ling's work schedule for "Scratch" left her with little time to engage in the usual pastimes of high school. Her hosting duties required her to travel constantly, and she admitted that she sometimes missed just hanging out with friends, going to high school sporting events, and other "normal" activities. "I sacrificed my whole junior and senior years," she acknowledged. "I mean, I still had a good time ... but at the same time, I missed a lot of school." But Ling also was quick to add that her early experiences with "Scratch" provided her with a foundation for much of her later success. "I learned to perform in front of the camera [on "Scratch"], and I was able to gain a lot of confidence from that," she said.

After graduating from high school in 1990, Ling continued to work on "Scratch." But a year later—having worked on the program for three years by that point—she made plans to leave the show and resume her education at Boston University. A few months before classes began, however, she received an intriguing phone call from New York City. The caller was a producer for Channel One, a

"There was a time when I wanted to do the whole acting thing, but then I started to get educated," Ling said. "I just decided that I wanted to pursue a career that will allow me to really utilize my mind.... I can't believe that I'm actually getting paid for getting fed knowledge. I'm learning so much every day, and I actually get paid for it."

satellite news service that broadcasts a daily news program to thousands of middle schools and high schools across the United States. The producer asked Ling if she was interested in auditioning for a reporter position with the channel.

Making Her Mark at Channel One

Ling turned in a terrific audition, and the Channel One producers offered her the opportunity to become the network's youngest news reporter. She quickly accepted, working at Channel One from 1991 to 1998. Ling spent seven years there delivering news stories that reached an estimated eight million student viewers on a daily basis. The experience convinced her to explore a career in journalism. "There was a time when I wanted to do the whole acting thing, but then I started to get educated," she said. "I just decided that I wanted to pursue a career that will allow me to really utilize my mind.… I can't believe that I'm actually getting paid for getting fed knowledge. I'm learning so much every day, and I actually get paid for it."

During her years at Channel One, Ling delivered reports from more than two dozen countries, including Vietnam, China, India, Iran, Iraq, and Japan. Some of these assignments, such as ones that had her report on drug cartels in Colombia and civil war in Afghanistan, placed her in personal danger. "I saw boys who looked about ten years old carrying weapons larger than they were," she recalled about her time in Afghanistan. "They had no light in their eyes; they looked like they could shoot me right then and there with no remorse whatsoever."

Carrying out these assignments would have exhausted most young reporters, but Ling's ambition, enthusiasm, and energy drove her to take on other challenges as well. For example, she took history classes at USC during her first few years at Channel One. She also found the time to help make eight documentary films with the local Public Broadcasting System (PBS) affiliate in Los Angeles during the 1990s. Ling admitted that managing her obligations as a student, reporter, and documentary filmmaker was "incredibly difficult. I'm up all the time till two in the morning doing papers. I rarely, rarely go out. I've almost completely eliminated my social life. But I have a really good time at work. It's fun. I don't think I'll regret anything because I don't think I've sacrificed anything. I can party all I want when I finish school.… I know that sounds weird that I actually like being at work. I really do."

Joining "The View"

In 1997 Ling entered an exciting new phase of her career when she reached an agreement with ABC News to deliver ten news feature stories for broadcast on national television. The work that she turned in for ABC over the next several months deeply impressed veteran ABC news journalist Barbara Walters. Intrigued by the smart but approachable image that the young journalist projected in her reports, Walters asked Ling if she would be interested in joining "The View," one of the nation's top-rated daytime talk shows. "The View" uses a format in which five women of different ages and backgrounds, led by Walters, informally discuss everything from breaking news stories to lighthearted family topics and celebrity gossip.

Walters explained that the show's producers wanted to find a fresh face to represent the perspective of America's "20-something" generation of

Ling on the set of Channel One in 1997. Her reports from around the world drew enthusiastic letters from students who were eager to learn about current events.

women. The woman they chose would join the other "View" hosts—Walters, Meredith Vieira, Star Jones, and Joy Behar—on broadcasts into American living rooms five days a week. The 25-year-old Ling jumped at

*Ling and her co-hosts from "The View" appearing at an awards show.
From left: Star Jones, Joy Behar, Barbara Walters, Ling, and Meredith Vieira.*

the invitation to audition, and she beat out more than 12,000 applicants for the job. According to the other hosts of "The View," selecting Ling was an easy decision. "She was very likable and she was smart but also adorable," said Vieira. "She wasn't a know-it-all but she knows a lot. She had it all and we just immediately clicked." Walters also sung her praises. "The number one thing was chemistry," she explained. "Lisa just seemed to fit with all of us … but she's also able to give her opinions. And she has opinions based on fact."

After joining "The View" in May 1999, Ling's public profile increased enormously. Ratings for the show soared, and television critics praised her friendly personality and her ability to stand her ground without offending her opinionated co-hosts. In 2000 she agreed to be a spokesperson in Old Navy television commercials, and she also became a regular contributor to the *USA Today* weekend magazine and the *New York Times* wire service.

Growing Restless

In 2000 Ling filled breaks in the taping schedule of "The View" with work on the College Television Network, a satellite television channel that reached an estimated two million students at colleges and universities all across the United States. She worked for the network as its senior political correspondent for the 2000 elections.

The excitement of reporting on important presidential and congressional elections reminded Ling of her journalistic experiences during her Channel One days. She realized that she missed the adventurous lifestyle of the international news reporter. Ling still enjoyed her work on "The View," but as the months passed she became increasingly restless. Her restlessness became even greater after the September 11, 2001, terrorist attacks on New York City and Washington DC. "That was really a pivotal moment that really propelled me to just want to get back in the world," she recalled. "I just felt like there weren't enough people asking why this happened."

In 2002 Ling's growing desire to find a new challenge led her to apply for the job of host of "National Geographic Ultimate Explorer," a program that appeared on Sunday nights on the MSNBC cable network. As host, she would get the opportunity to travel to exotic and fascinating places around the world and "cover the world and all that's in it," in the words of Alexander Graham Bell, one of the founders of the National Geographic Society.

> *According to the other hosts of "The View," selecting Ling was an easy decision. "The number one thing was chemistry," Walters explained. "Lisa just seemed to fit with all of us ... but she's also able to give her opinions. And she has opinions based on fact."*

Ling was awarded the job, and she made her last hosting appearance on "The View" on December 5, 2002. All of her colleagues wished her well, and she expressed appreciation to them for being both friends and mentors to her. Looking back, though, Ling had no regrets about the decision. "['The View'] raised my profile a lot," she admitted, "but it's not where you want to spend the rest of your career."

Exploring the Globe

Ling approached her new job as host of "National Geographic Ultimate Explorer" with a tremendous feeling of excitement and anticipation. She knew that it was a once-in-a-lifetime opportunity. "I'm not married and I don't have kids," she said. "If I don't do this now, I don't know if I could do it in a couple of years." Ling's first reports began airing in May 2003. Over

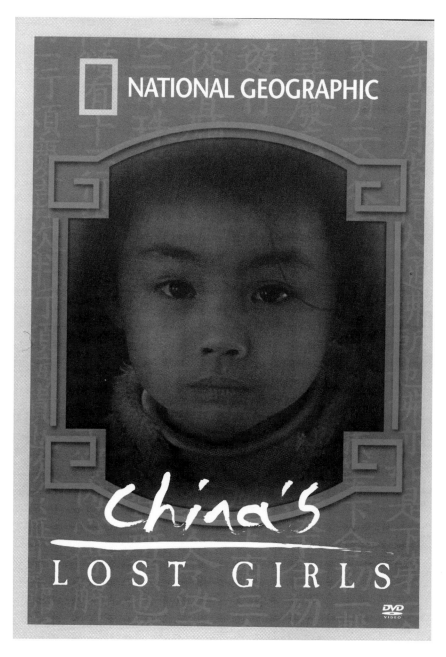

On "China's Lost Girls," an episode in the series "National Geographic Ultimate Explorer," Ling examined the issues surrounding the country's one-child policy and its impact on Chinese society—especially on girls.

the next several months, viewers watched her report on topics ranging from the black market trade in Tibetan antelope hides to the violence and looting that wracked Baghdad following the 2003 U.S.-led invasion of Iraq.

Ling also confirmed that she had made the right choice in leaving "The View" and joining "National Geographic Ultimate Explorer." "Here, we work weeks—if not months—exploring one topic," she explained. "Having a discussion about Tom Cruise's backside versus jumping out of cranes and rolling around on the ground in the middle of forest fires—while both are thoroughly engaging, there's no question which story is meatier." She also claimed that her hosting job was more rewarding than those offered by more powerful and famous news organizations. "Network news covers international stories when there is catastrophe or war, but there are so many other rich, appealing stories out there," Ling stated. "One reason I love National Geographic so much is that they take a risk. They cover stories not because they think it will rate hugely but because they really are compelling, interesting, educational stories."

In January 2005 Ling's program was renamed "Explorer" and made the centerpiece of the new National Geographic Channel. These changes did not alter the show's emphasis on world exploration, though. "Before I got the job at "Explorer," I was living in New York seven days a week," stated Ling. "Now I'm out of the country every month: I was in China in February, Mexico in March, Japan and Korea in April, and Israel and Russia in May and June."

In addition, Ling's assignments remained just as exciting and unpredictable as ever. The show has taken her to Colombia, where she reported on that country's problems with violent drug cartels. She also went to China to examine that country's controversial "one-child" family planning policy, which has resulted in countless unwanted female babies since Chinese culture values male children more. She also traveled to Chechnya and

"Network news covers international stories when there is catastrophe or war, but there are so many other rich, appealing stories out there," Ling stated. "One reason I love National Geographic so much is that they take a risk. They cover stories not because they think it will rate hugely but because they really are compelling, interesting, educational stories."

the Middle East to report on female suicide bombers. In addition, Ling also explored the dangerous culture inside American prisons and the vicious behavior of El Salvador street gangs. She even used a medical technician disguise to record and smuggle footage out of the secretive Communist country of North Korea.

Special Correspondent for "Oprah"

In keeping with her history, though, Ling did not permit her hectic "Explorer" schedule to keep her from pursuing other interests. For example, she dedicated much of her rare free time to an intensive study of her family's genealogy or family tree. "Looking back at my heritage, I've learned that the values that my family lived by have become a part of me," she said. "And their struggles as immigrants taught me to appreciate what it means to be American, without forgetting what it means to be Chinese." Ling's interest in genealogy even led her to write the 2005 book, *Mother, Daughter, Sister, Bride: Rituals of Womanhood,* in which she blends an account of her family's history with discussions of the rites of passage experienced by women all around the world.

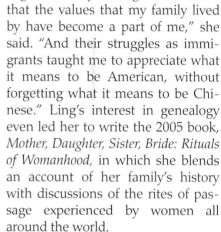

"Looking back at my heritage, I've learned that the values that my family lived by have become a part of me," Ling said. "And their struggles as immigrants taught me to appreciate what it means to be American, without forgetting what it means to be Chinese."

In 2005 Ling also began working as a special correspondent for "The Oprah Winfrey Show." This arrangement has given her the opportunity to put together detailed reports on such troubling subjects as the toll of AIDS and civil war in various parts of Africa. Ling has acknowledged that some of the stories are grim and depressing, but she thinks that people have to become more emotionally engaged about the suffering and injustice that surrounds them. "I've been so disenchanted with the apathy amongst young people for what's going on around the world," she said. "Our generation will inevitably assume the problems our country is faced with, and we are so ill-equipped to do so. My hope is that I can somehow raise the level of consciousness about world events."

To this end, in 2007 Ling launched a documentary series called "Who Cares about Girls?" on the Oxygen cable television network. The individ-

On a report in the documentary series "Who Cares about Girls," Ling drew attention to the many poor girls in India who are forced into prostitution to earn money for their families.

ual reports in this series all share the same basic goal: to educate viewers about the different challenges confronting women in America and around the world. One early report in the series, for example, looked at women in the U.S. prison system, showing the difficulties that imprisoned mothers have maintaining relationships with their children on the outside. Another story concerned the thousands of poor girls in India who are forced into prostitution to support their families.

Ling hopes that American families will gather together to watch the reports that she prepares for National Geographic, Oxygen, and "The Oprah Winfrey Show." "These are real stories about real people, and I think kids should be exposed to it, especially American kids who are, in many cases, very entitled and impervious to what happens in the world," she explained. "Honestly, there's a lot of stuff on TV, people have a lot of options, but I truly hope that people watch and respond to this, because only if people watch and respond will we be able to continue doing these stories. Otherwise, the little voice I'm giving them will disappear."

No Plans to Slow Down

Ling has occasionally taken a break from her more serious work to take on fun, glamorous jobs such as interviewing celebrities at the Academy Awards. "I am very proud that most of my work is very serious," she said. "But you know, I'm a girl and I sometimes like to ask girlie things, and I don't think that jeopardizes my ability to do quality journalism at all."

> *"I love what I'm doing now," Ling revealed. "And I've never been this way before. I've always wanted to figure out what the next step should be, what ladder to climb and to what end. Now I love what I do and I'm praying to God it doesn't go away soon."*

Ling insists that she will never waste her time and talent reporting on the tabloid trials and celebrity scandals that major news media outlets cover so heavily. "We have soldiers dying every day," she declared. "[Excessive coverage of those kinds of stories] doesn't sit well with me. I also don't want to sound like this nerdy activist. But to me it's just sort of a sad commentary on the culture."

With this in mind, Ling has said that she hopes to continue hosting "Explorer" and working on other noteworthy projects for years to come. "I love what I'm doing now," she revealed. "And I've never been this way before. I've always wanted to figure out what the next step should be, what ladder to climb and to what end. Now I love what I do and I'm praying to God it doesn't go away soon."

MARRIAGE AND FAMILY

Ling married Paul Song, a doctor who specializes in the treatment of cancerous tumors, in Los Angeles, California, on May 26, 2007.

HOBBIES AND OTHER INTERESTS

Despite her busy and successful career, Ling has always remembered the things in life that are of lasting importance, such as family ties. In April 2001, for example, she decided to race in the Boston Marathon as part of an effort to raise money and awareness for the Ali & Dad's Army Foundation. This pediatric cancer research foundation had been founded in memory of Ling's cousin, Ali Pierce, who died of liver cancer at age 13. A short time after founding the charity, though, Ali's father (and Ling's uncle) died of a heart attack while running a mini-marathon. Ling decided to run the Boston Marathon as a way to honor her uncle, her cousin, and the good work of the charity. Even though she had only had a few short months to train, Ling managed to finish the 26-mile marathon in four hours and 34 minutes.

When enjoying one of her rare breaks from her work on "Explorer" and other programs, Ling likes to read, listen to music, and practice yoga.

SELECTED CREDITS

Television

"Scratch," 1989-1991
"Channel One," 1991-1998
"The View," 1999-2002
"National Geographic Ultimate Explorer," 2002-present (renamed "Explorer" in 2005)

WRITINGS

Mother, Daughter, Sister, Bride: Rituals of Womanhood, 2005 (with Joanne Eicher)

FURTHER READING

Books

Ling, Lisa, with Joanne Eicher. *Mother, Daughter, Sister, Bride: Rituals of Womanhood,* 2005

Periodicals

Daily News of Los Angeles, Mar. 22, 2007, p.U7
In Style, Mar. 2001, p.470
Los Angeles Times, Nov. 13, 1997, p.F50; Mar. 5, 2007, p.E3
New York Daily News, May 25, 1999; May 26, 1999
New York Post, Aug. 8, 1999, p.110
People, May 24, 1999; Dec. 2, 2002, p. 24; Aug. 25, 2003, p.79
Philadelphia Daily News, Aug. 2, 1999, p.39
Psychology Today, Jan. 1, 2003, p.37
Television Week, Jan. 5, 2004, p.7
Time, May 22, 2000, p.126
Transpacific, June 1994, p.18

Online Articles

http://www.nationalgeographic.com/adventure/0412/excerpt5.html
  (National Geographic Adventure Magazine, "Lisa Ling Changes Channels," Dec. 2004/Jan. 2005)

ADDRESS

Lisa Ling
National Geographic Society
P.O. Box 98199
Washington, DC 20090-8199

WORLD WIDE WEB SITES

http://www.abc.com/theview/hosts/ling.html
http://www.channel.nationalgeographic.com/channel/explorer

Christina Norman 1963-
American Media Executive
President of MTV

BIRTH

Christina Norman was born on July 30, 1963, in New York, New York. She was raised by her father and her mother, and she has one brother. Her family is Hispanic and African American.

YOUTH

Norman grew up in working-class neighborhoods in the South Bronx and Queens, two sections of New York City. Her father was passionate about music, spending a lot of his free time listening to jazz and classical recordings. Her parents were serious enough about music to invest in a piano and send both their children to piano lessons. Sometimes her mother would take Christina along to the office building where she worked as an administrative assistant. Through such outings, Norman remembered, "I learned how to carry myself in a corporate setting." She also watched a lot of television during the 1970s and 1980s, something that would serve her well later in life.

EDUCATION

Asked to give one word to describe herself in high school, Norman said: "Goofy." At the time, according to Norman, "I thought I would have some sort of creative pursuit. I didn't know *how* I'd do that exactly but I knew I wanted to contribute something in that way." After graduating from high school, she attended Boston University, where she earned a degree in film production during the mid-1980s.

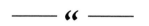

In high school, according to Norman, "I thought I would have some sort of creative pursuit. I didn't know how *I'd do that exactly but I knew I wanted to contribute something in that way."*

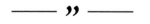

FIRST JOBS

In 1985, after graduating from college, Norman took a job in the Boston area with a small company that produced television commercials. She was hired as a production assistant, and her specialty was the "tabletop shot," in which the camera focuses exclusively on the product that is the subject of the advertisement. As simple as that sounds, it can be very difficult to do properly. Even though the tabletop shot is recognized as a vitally important part of a successful advertisement, it is one of the least creative parts of the entire commercial production. Setting up the tabletop shot and making it look just right requires a great deal of time and patience.

Her job had its tedious moments, but Norman liked it, especially when she compared it to the corporate jobs many of her friends were taking. "It was really freeing," she said. "A lot of my friends were going to work for Raytheon and Digital Equipment and those kinds of tech companies. I was, like, this is much better than having to do that." She also found working in media quite unusual compared to the role models she had when growing up. "A good job was a teacher, a nurse and, if you were lucky, a lawyer. But television was not a career choice in those days."

Still, she admitted that at times the boring aspects of her job did bother her. "I still remember my last spot," Norman recalled. "It was for Tylenol Allergy Sinus. It was all night shooting because the pill was the wrong color and we were using a motion control camera, which takes forever to set up." For a while, she thought about going into the film industry and making movies instead of advertisements. Eventually she decided against it. Instead, she moved from Boston back to New York City, where she continued doing production work on a freelance basis.

According to Tom Freston, chairman and chief executive officer of MTV Networks, "Christina is a most gifted, creative executive and has helped make MTV just about the smartest and most distinctive network out there."

During the late 1980s, Norman heard of a job opening at MTV. Debuting in 1981, MTV was a cable television network broadcasting music videos, which were still a relatively new phenomenon at that time. Norman eagerly interviewed for a staff position at the network. She did not get the job, but she soon had a chance to do some work for the company as a freelance production coordinator. This gave her the opportunity to prove her skills and competence to those in charge at MTV. They continued to use Norman for freelance work until 1991, when she was hired as a full-time staff member. In her new position as a production manager, she worked on promotional material related to MTV and its programming.

CAREER HIGHLIGHTS

"Beavis and Butt-Head" Provides Norman's First Big Break

In 1993, Norman's supervisor at MTV came through the office asking if anyone there had any experience with animation. Employees were being recruited to work on a new animated series. Norman immediately volunteered, even though she had no previous experience with animation at all. "I can figure anything out," she thought at the time. Her confidence paid off. The new program was "Beavis and Butt-Head," which focused on two teenaged boys, their crude humor, and their relentless ridiculing of old MTV videos. The show was heavily promoted through the advertising campaign

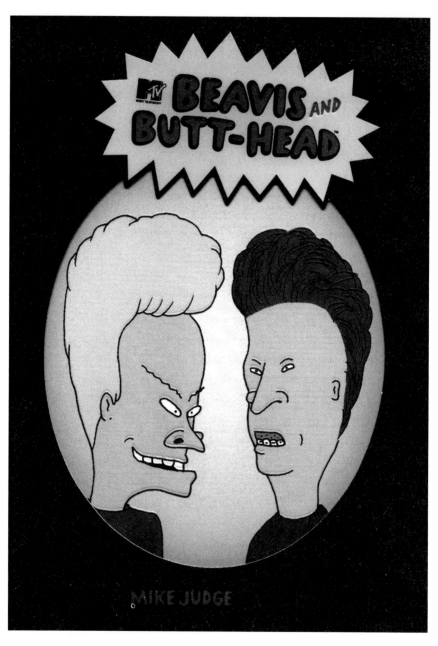

Norman's promotional campaign for "Beavis and Butt-Head"
was her first big success.

Norman helped design, and once it began airing, "Beavis and Butt-Head" became a huge success. It was one of the top-rated programs on MTV and gave rise to "Beavis and Butt-Head" clothing, toys, games, and more.

Following her triumph with "Beavis and Butt-Head," Norman rose steadily through the ranks at MTV. She became supervising producer of on-air promotions, director of on-air promotions, senior vice-president of promotions, and finally in 1999, senior vice-president of marketing and on-air promotions. In 2002, she was in charge of the marketing campaign for "The Osbournes," a quirky reality show featuring the life of aging rocker Ozzy Osbourne (from the band Black Sabbath) and his offbeat family. "The Osbournes" was another big success, attracting an audience far beyond MTV's usual viewers. During its first season, "The Osbournes" won the highest television ratings of any show ever aired on the MTV network.

Jump-Starting VH1

During the 1990s, Norman had proven her leadership ability. Under her direction, MTV won many awards for its advertising, promotion, and design. She had shown she was able to be creative, to inspire creativity in those working for her, and to lead and guide her employees to work together as a team. Her success caught the attention of Judy McGrath, who was then president of MTV Networks Music Group and was later promoted to chief executive officer of MTV Networks. McGrath decided that Norman's strengths were needed at MTV's sister network, Video Hits 1 (VH1). (For more information on Judy McGrath, see *Biography Today Business Leaders*, Vol. 1.)

VH1 had been founded in 1985, four years after MTV's debut. While MTV was aimed primarily at a teen audience, VH1 was designed for those in an older age bracket. Instead of the cutting-edge image of MTV, VH1 featured softer pop sounds from established adult-contemporary artists. "Behind the Music," a documentary series, gave in-depth looks at the stories behind the popular artists and bands featured on the network. VH1 was a great success for its first several years, but in 2000, ratings for the music network began a nosedive. The decline continued until 2002, leaving VH1 trailing far behind MTV in popularity.

McGrath wanted to turn that situation around. She created a new position, that of general manager of VH1, and offered it to Norman, who accepted it. In announcing Norman's new position, McGrath said, "Christina is a tremendously creative executive who has a great strategic understanding for connecting with consumers, combined with a great feel for how to brand and position a network. In her 11 years at MTV, she's proven to be a fantastic leader of creative people—cultivating an environment where they

"The Osbournes" was another big success for Norman.

can produce their absolute best work." Praise also came from Tom Freston, chairman and chief executive officer of MTV Networks. He commented, "I can't think of a better choice to lead VH1 into the future. Christina is a most gifted, creative executive and has helped make MTV just about the smartest and most distinctive network out there."

Norman's first move was to spend some time with her executive team discussing the challenges facing VH1. They identified a few problems that were hurting the cable channel. The network had been relying too much on old material like "Behind the Music," which had grown stale. At the same time, there was an atmosphere in the VH1 offices that discouraged new ideas. "Morale was really down. Everyone was waiting around for permission," Norman said. "The VH1 team had become a little discouraged during a tough time. They really just needed to sort of regain their footing and work together in a new way than they had. Once they trusted themselves again, great ideas could bubble up and make it successful again." Norman encouraged everyone at VH1 to take risks and throw out all the new ideas they could, as they sought ways to make the network feel fresh and exciting again. "For me, it was all about making VH1 live," she said.

> *"Music education isn't just important to VH1," Norman said. "It should be important to everyone. Studies have shown that music education builds brain-power. We feel that restoring music programs in public schools across the country is helping kids do better in school."*

While trying to dispel the image of the network as a dry, dull music archive, Norman also made it clear from the start that she and VH1 were committed to music education. The network's Save the Music campaign utilized fund-raising concerts and public-service announcements to support music programs in public schools. "Music education isn't just important to VH1," she said. "It should be important to everyone. Studies have shown that music education builds brain-power. We feel that restoring music programs in public schools across the country is helping kids do better in school."

New Energy and New Ideas

VH1's makeover included new on-air graphics, new set designs, new programming, and new advertising. A Pop-Art style was adopted, based on the work of artists from the 1950s and 1960s. Probably the best-known artist in the Pop movement was Andy Warhol. He and others in the Pop Art school used images from popular culture and advertising in their works, rather than images from religion or nature, which had inspired the art of earlier eras. Andy Warhol's repeating patterns of soup cans, or his silkscreen prints of famous faces, are among the best-known examples of Pop Art. At VH1, the Pop Art style showed a new willingness to be playful rather than stuffy and self-important.

The network extended this fun, fresh feeling with new programs that focused on nostalgia for the recent past. "I Love the '80s" was a fast-paced program featuring clips from music and TV from the 1980s, mixed with footage of contemporary interviews with the stars of that time. "Bands Reunited" brought together members of defunct bands in an interview format. A comedy show, "Best Week Ever," gave various comedians a chance to comment on the newsworthy events of the preceding week. Other new shows included "Driven," which exposed the ambitions of stars, and "Inside Out," a reality show that exposed the everyday lives of musicians. "I Love the '80s" gave rise to successful spinoffs, "I Love the '70s" and "I Love the '90s."

Not every program started during this period was a success. "Music Behind Bars," a reality show about rock bands formed by prison inmates, was canceled after complaints from the families of crime victims. Another highly-publicized reality show was developed to give an inside look into the celebrity marriage of Liza Minnelli and David Gest, but the couple broke up before the show could be produced.

Despite those failed programs, Norman's changes were overwhelmingly effective. VH1 became very popular once again. In fact, under Norman's leadership, ratings for the network increased by 80 percent, climbing to the highest levels VH1 had ever reached. Her success led to her being honored as one of *Ebony* magazine's Top 10 African-Americans in Television for 2002. In 2003 she was recognized by *Crain's New York Business* as one of the Top 40 under 40 Businesspeople in New York, and by *Hollywood Reporter* as one of the Power 100 Women in Entertainment. In January 2004, McGrath promoted Norman to the position of president of VH1. As she took on her new job, Norman became one of the most influential women of color in the television industry.

Leading MTV into the 21st Century

Norman's term of service at VH1 was significant, but short. In 2005, McGrath asked her to come back to MTV, this time as the network's president.

As president of MTV, Norman often meets with music celebrities, including (from left) T.I., Beyoncé, and Justin Timberlake.

MTV had changed drastically since it was founded in 1981. By this time the main cable channel was focused more on original programming than music videos. Yet MTV had become much more than merely a single cable channel. The network now had many faces, based on evolving technologies. MTV was available not only on cable television networks, but also on the Internet and wireless mobile platforms. It had developed numerous ways to fine-tune and deliver its product, and McGrath wanted someone in charge who would strengthen and continue MTV's progressive growth.

As president, Norman took over a wide range of responsibilities. They included overseeing business development, research, communications, marketing, and finance. She was responsible for guiding not only MTV but many of its offshoots, which include MTV2, which plays more music than the original station; MTV Tr3s, designed to reach a young Hispanic audience; MTVu, a college service; and other MTV offshoots such as MTV Chi, MTVK, and MTV Desi, which are available online and are designed to appeal to Chinese Americans, Koreans, and South Asians. As she told an interviewer, "Reaching out to multicultural audiences, I believe, will be a hallmark of the Christina Norman era."

In addition to fine-tuning these specialized offerings, Norman also supervised the digital networks MTV Hits and MTV Jams, as well as the popular

MTV.com and MTV Overdrive broadband service. Overall, the MTV brand has grown to include more than 50 television channels in 28 languages, seen in 168 countries. When all its applications are considered, MTV reaches into 88 million homes in the United States and 442 million homes around the globe.

The MTV empire is vast, but Norman proved she had the vision necessary to manage it. In 2006, she announced that MTV would be restructured into two units or "ecosystems." One would focus on short-form content to be broadcast on television, on-line, and mobile sources. The other would be devoted to producing long-form entertainment, such as reality television shows. Remarking on the fast-changing technological possibilities, Norman said, "I think there's a lot of experimentation, which is a good thing because I think that's what fuels MTV and will continue to fuel MTV."

> ——— " ———
>
> *"Every generation of young people has chafed against the world they've inherited.... It's our mission at MTV and our privilege to focus that revolutionary energy and to build tomorrow's leaders. Now, we do it all through a three-step mantra: engage, educate, and empower."*
>
> ——— " ———

Also in 2006, Norman announced MTV's new social awareness program, Break the Addiction. This public-service effort encourages young people to combat global warming by using less oil. "The spirit of rebellion is part of our rock and roll DNA," she announced. "Every generation of young people has chafed against the world they've inherited.... It's our mission at MTV and our privilege to focus that revolutionary energy and to build tomorrow's leaders. Now, we do it all through a three-step mantra: engage, educate, and empower. Engage young people on the issues they care about. Educate them about those issues. And empower them to take action that's going to make a difference."

New Opportunities

Despite all her corporate responsibilities, Norman still makes sure to stay in touch with MTV's primary audience. "We spend a lot of time talking to young people on-line, in person—it's what we do," she said. "[It's] our mission." She also emphasizes that in the 21st century, "MTV is not a cable network." With cable being just one of its methods of delivering its content, new ways of reaching and serving audiences continue to evolve as technology expands. Norman is committed to making the best use of new technologies and making sure that MTV stays up-to-the-minute. In England, MTV is experimenting with new ideas such as Flux, an online application that combines traditional MTV content with features from other popular online sites like YouTube and MySpace.

Reflecting on the future of MTV, Norman said, "We've got this incredible collection of assets, starting with the big channel of MTV and going down to mobile and MTV2 and all the new channels. How are we going to make sure that all of those are presenting and creating a unique experience for the audience? That's job one every day: making sure the audience is connected to the music and the artists and the shows that they love."

Norman remains committed to helping educate, as well as entertain, young people. She is active in PENCIL (Public Education Needs Civic Involvement in Learning), an organization that gets the business world involved in public school education. PENCIL generates millions of dollars in donations to public schools each year. It also sponsors the Principal for a Day program, in which business executives come to public schools and act as principals for one day. Norman has taken her turn as Principal for a Day and strongly supports the program.

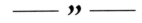

"We've got this incredible collection of assets, starting with the big channel of MTV and going down to mobile and MTV2 and all the new channels. How are we going to make sure that all of those are presenting and creating a unique experience for the audience? That's job one every day: making sure the audience is connected to the music and the artists and the shows that they love."

Norman gave part of the credit for her success to the cable television industry. "The cable industry is friendly to women, probably I would assume because in its infancy it paid less and jobs were plentiful. And that I think attracted more women to it," she said. "Throughout this whole organization, not just MTV, but Viacom, there's a lot of women in charge." Referring to Judy McGrath, Norman added, "I came here when Judy was president, and that was definitely one of the things that kept me here.... It was inspiring and motivating.... She was very who she was, and that sort of makes you comfortable being who you are. And know that you can succeed."

When MTV and MySpace hosted the "Presidential Dialogue Series" with Barack Obama, Norman posed with Obama (center), Ian Rowe from MTV (left), and Jeff Berman and Liba Rubenstein from MySpace (right).

Norman urged young women to take themselves seriously. "Speak up for yourself because you *are* valid. Your needs are valid, what you want is valid, and what you give is valid. You've got to find a way to use your voice to get what you need. But it's not just running off at the mouth. A lot of people talk but don't have anything to contribute. So learn when to listen and when to talk.... There are interns who say they want to be me. But I'm like, 'Be great at *you* first. Then you can be somebody else.' You have to be the best *you* you can be."

MARRIAGE AND FAMILY

Christina Norman is married to Charles Hunt, and the couple has two daughters, Zoe and Asha. The family lives in Brooklyn, New York. "I love spending time with my family," Norman said. "Outside of work, my complete and total devotion is to them."

HOBBIES AND OTHER INTERESTS

Norman loves to cook, ice skate, and go in-line skating.

HONORS AND AWARDS

One of the Top 10 African-Americans in Television (*Ebony*): 2002
Emmy Award for National Public Service: 2002
One of the Top 40 under 40 Businesspeople in New York (*Crain's New York Business*): 2003
One of the Power 100 Women in Entertainment (*Hollywood Reporter*): 2003
Quasar Vision Award (National Association for Multi-Ethnicity in Communications): 2003
Diversity List of Most Powerful Businesspeople of Color (*Fortune*): 2005
Entertainment Marketing Award (*Ebony* magazine): 2005
One of Cable Television's Most Powerful Women (*Cableworld*): 2006
One of the Top 25 New York Latino Movers and Shakers (*New York Post*): 2006

FURTHER READING

Periodicals

Billboard, Aug. 27, 2005, p.23
Broadcasting & Cable, June 16, 2003, p.42; Mar. 14, 2005, p.7; May 16, 2005, p.4
CosmoGIRL!, June 1, 2006, p.122
Current Biography Yearbook, 2007
Daily Variety, Apr. 19, 2002, p.1
Miami Herald, Aug. 27, 2005
Multichannel News, Jan. 30, 2006, p.A20

Online Articles

http://www.hollywoodreporter.com
(Hollywood Reporter, "Rock Chick-MTV at 25," June 2, 2006)
http://www.npr.org,
(National Public Radio, "From Upstart to Parent Network," Aug. 1, 2006)

ADDRESS

Christina Norman
MTV
1515 Broadway
23rd Floor
New York, NY 10036

WORLD WIDE WEB SITES

http://www.mtv.com

Rihanna 1988-

Barbadian Singer
Performer of the Hit Songs "Pon de Replay,"
"S.O.S." and "Umbrella"

BIRTH

Rihanna was born Robyn Rihanna Fenty in St. Michael, Barbados, on February 20, 1988 (some sources say February 18). Barbados is an island nation located in the southeastern Caribbean region with strong ties to Great Britain. Rihanna is of mixed Irish and Guyanese ancestry, with a black mother and a biracial father. Her mother, Monica Fenty, worked as an accountant and now owns a clothing store. Her father, Ronald

Fenty, is employed by a clothing manufacturer. Rihanna has two younger brothers, Rajad and Rorrey.

YOUTH

Rihanna has said that her early life was often troubled by unhappy incidents associated with her father's substance abuse problems. He has since recovered. At the time, however, his use of alcohol, crack cocaine, and marijuana disrupted the household and caused problems for the family. Rihanna experienced severe headaches that persisted until her parents divorced when she was 14 years old.

——— **"** ———

From an early age, Rihanna recalled, "I just knew that I loved music, and I developed a passion for it. I really, really wanted to become a singer from a very young age."

——— **"** ———

Still, during her free time Rihanna enjoyed island life. She played with her brothers and their friends more than with dolls or other girls. According to Rihanna, "I was more of a tomboy, so I'd climb trees and come home all scratched up." She loved singing and dancing, too. She recalled, "I just knew that I loved music, and I developed a passion for it. I really, really wanted to become a singer from a very young age." However, she only sang in the shower or in front of a mirror in her bedroom. "I would hold a broom like a mike stand.… My neighbors would complain—they always knew when I was home." Rihanna first performed publicly in 2004, when she appeared in a high school talent show. She sang Mariah Carey's "Hero" in the school competition and won. At about the same time she won a local beauty contest and formed a trio with two of her friends.

EDUCATION

Rihanna attended Charles F. Broome Memorial elementary school and Combermere secondary school, which is equivalent to high school in the United States. She left school before graduating in order to pursue her singing career. After that, she was home schooled to complete her education.

CAREER HIGHLIGHTS

In December 2003, when Rihanna was 15 years old, a friend introduced her to record producer Evan Rogers, who had worked with such recording artists as Christina Aguilera, Kelly Clarkson, and Jessica Simpson. Rogers was vacationing in Barbados with his wife, a native of the island, when Rihanna auditioned for him at the hotel where he was staying. Based on that performance, Rogers introduced her to Carl Sturken, his partner in the production company SRP Records. The pair invited her to record with them in New York. During breaks from school Rihanna traveled to the United States and began working on recordings for a demo CD. Among the songs on the disc was the original version of "Pon de Replay," which would become her first international hit.

As soon as Rihanna completed the demo recording, she returned to Barbados. In the meantime Rogers sent the disc to several record companies. Def Jam Recordings was the first to call him—the very next day—to set up a live audition for Rihanna with Def Jam president Jay-Z (Shawn Carter). Rihanna flew back to the United States and within 24 hours was in Jay-Z's office in New York performing for him and a small group of record company executives and lawyers. She later recalled the whirlwind speed of the event. "I left to go back to Barbados from New York on the Monday. The demo was sent in on Wednesday, Def Jam called back

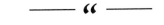

Jay-Z later commented in **Rolling Stone,** *"I signed her in one day.... It took me two minutes to see she was a star."*

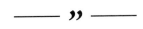

Thursday, and the producers went over for a meeting, so I had to come back on Friday evening. I was supposed to come back on my next school holiday in February but the guys over at Def Jam said, 'Why do you have to wait?' That's when I knew it was serious."

The audition so impressed Jay-Z and Def Jam that they told Rihanna's representatives to cancel her auditions for other companies, and they worked out an agreement on the spot. That same night, Rihanna signed a contract to record six CDs for the label. She was just 16 years old. Jay-Z later commented in *Rolling Stone,* "I signed her in one day.... It took me two minutes to see she was a star."

Music of the Sun

Rihanna's first album, *Music of the Sun* (2005), combines urban dance pop, rhythm and blues, and reggae with straightforward pop ballads that showcase her vocal talents and her island charm. The biggest hit on the album was the dance anthem "Pon de Replay," cowritten by Rogers and Sturken,

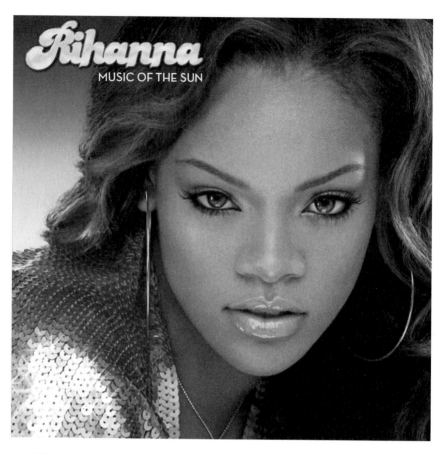

Rihanna released her first CD, Music of the Sun, *when she was just 17.*

along with Vada Nobles and Alisha Brooks. Released as a single in June 2005, "Pon de Replay" became a chart-topping international hit that summer. It was the first song of her own that Rihanna ever heard on the radio. She recalled, "My mom and I were in a mall. The deejay had given me a heads-up that he was going to play it, so I bought a handheld radio, and I was listening to it all day. When it came on, I just started screaming with my mom."

"Pon de replay" is a Barbadian dialect phrase meaning "play it again." She explained the expression, saying, "It's just language that we speak in Barbados. It's broken English. Pon is *on*, De means *the*, so it's just basically telling the DJ to put my song on the replay." In the song Rihanna repeatedly urges a deejay to "turn the music up." *People* reviewer Chuck Arnold noted that with "its infectious, hand-clapping dancehall groove, Rihanna's smash 'Pon de Replay' has indeed had deejays turning the music up, over and over." Mark Medina, the program director of a radio station in Phoenix, Arizona, called "Pon de Replay" "a good summer song.... You kind of get into the rhythm of it and it jumps off the dial."

With the worldwide success of her first release, Rihanna embarked on a concert tour as the opening act for singer Gwen Stefani. Initially, some critics believed that Rihanna would not be able to sustain the level of success that she attained with her first album. Others compared her to the American pop and R&B superstar Beyoncé Knowles, who rose to fame in the 1990s as the lead singer of the group Destiny's Child. Rihanna found the comparison flattering at first because she was a fan of Beyoncé, but it became frustrating as she struggled to create her own musical identity. As she later said, "it does get a little upsetting when people say I copy her."

Before long Rihanna was in the studio again, working on her second album, *A Girl Like Me* (2006). By summer she had another international success with the single "S.O.S." from her new album. "S.O.S." grabs listeners' attention with the repeated use of a sampled beat from the 1981 megahit "Tainted Love" by the British duo Soft Cell. In the song Rihanna fuses a Caribbean dance groove with 1980s power pop. "'S.O.S.' talks about being rescued from a crazy feeling, calling out for help," she explained. "You know like when you have a huge crush on a guy, come rescue me from feeling this crazy." The single topped the *Billboard* Pop, Dance, and Hot 100 charts in the United States, surpassing the earlier success of "Pon de Replay."

> **"**
>
> *The first time Rihanna heard one of her songs on the radio, "My mom and I were in a mall. The deejay had given me a heads-up that he was going to play it, so I bought a handheld radio, and I was listening to it all day. When it came on, I just started screaming with my mom."*
>
> **"**

In support of *A Girl Like Me*, Rihanna toured during 2006 with such acts as Jay-Z and Ne-Yo in Australia and with the Pussycat Dolls in the United Kingdom. She soon released a second single from the album, the ballad "Unfaithful," a song written by her friend Ne-Yo. "Unfaithful" tells the story of a woman who regrets cheating on a good man. Critics noted that the song showcased a different aspect of Rihanna as a performer who could sing with emotion rather than just produce danceable pop tunes. Reviewer Clover Hope commented in *Billboard* that "['Unfaithful'] ultimately reveals a promising young vocalist growing into her own."

For the third single from *A Girl Like Me*, Rihanna chose "We Ride." The song tells a story very different from the one in "Unfaithful." According to Rihanna, "'We Ride' is about this guy saying over and over again, 'When we ride, we ride, we're gonna be together until the day that we die'—promising all these things.... And then it turns out he broke all of his promises."

Good Girl Gone Bad

Rihanna's third album, *Good Girl Gone Bad*, was released in June 2007, less than two years after her first CD. The rapid pace with which she produced new recordings drew comments from music writers, who noted that artists often wait two to three years between CDs in order to maximize sales. But Rihanna confessed to having workaholic tendencies. "I just love making music and the label loves to put me in the studio, so that always works great together." Antonio "L.A." Reid, chairman of the Island Def Jam Music Group, characterized Rihanna as an exceptionally dedicated performer. He told *Jet*, "Since the day that Rihanna was signed to the label, I don't recall her ever not working.... I don't recall her ever taking time off for anything, whether it is personal or whatever. We've always had scheduling nightmares because this woman works so hard. She's absolutely one of the hardest-working artists I've ever met or been involved with at any level."

Good Girl Gone Bad presented Rihanna as a more mature, edgy artist. She explained the title as referring to attitude, not behavior. In order to emphasize the break with her previous records, she transformed her appearance for the promotional tour introducing the record. She wore black leather clothing, dyed her hair black, and had her hair cut in a short, jagged bob. According to Rihanna, "My new look is purposely adult.... I wanted to show growth as a person and artist. But for me, 'bad girl' does not mean 'wild girl.' It's more about taking chances, trying new things—visually and musically."

In spring 2007 Rihanna had her biggest success yet with the release of "Umbrella," the lead single from *Good Girl Gone Bad*. The song reached No. 1 on the charts in numerous countries around the world, including the United States, United Kingdom, Canada, and Australia. The song was cowritten and produced by Jay-Z, who also performed on the song. "'Umbrella' is about being there for the ones you love," Rihanna said, "whether it is a friend, family, or a boyfriend, the song is basically saying no matter what, I'll be there for you. We all have and need those friends in our lives!" In December 2007 the song was nominated for two Grammy Awards, for song of the year and for record of the year.

Rihanna had a string of hits with her third release, Good Girl Gone Bad.

In addition to collaborating with Jay-Z and Ne-Yo on the album, Rihanna also worked with Justin Timberlake, who cowrote the ballad "Rehab," and with Timbaland (Timothy Z. Mosley), who performed with Rihanna on that track. As Timberlake told *Entertainment Weekly*, "[Rihanna is] a young artist stepping into the adult world.... To me, that song is the bridge for her to be accepted as an adult in the music industry."

The single "Shut Up and Drive," written by Rogers and Sturken, was released in June 2007. In the accompanying video Rihanna was shown working in an all-female auto shop and waving the checkered flag to start a race between two rival drivers. In *Billboard* Chuck Taylor asserted that with such hits "Rihanna and an able collaborative stable have catapulted a potential one-trick dancehall diva to the most dexterous singer of the decade's second half."

Several songs on *Good Girl Gone Bad* describe relationship troubles, including the title track "Good Girl Gone Bad" and "Let Me Get That."

"Breaking Dishes" is a revenge song sung by a woman waiting for an un-faithful man to come home. It includes the lines, "I am killing time, you know bleaching your clothes / I am roasting marshmallows on the fire / And what I am burning is your attire." But there are also danceable club hits, such as "Don't Stop the Music," a song about meeting a new guy at a disco. The song samples Michael Jackson's "Wanna Be Startin' Somethin'" (1982) with Rihanna repeating the African chant made famous by Jackson: "Mama-se, mama-sa, ma-ma-koo-sa." "Don't Stop the Music" was nominated for a Grammy Award as the best dance recording of 2007. Rihanna related her ability to create hit dance music to her own love of dance. "I love to dance and love seeing people dance. I'm from Barbados—it's all about rhythm and groove."

> "Since the day that Rihanna was signed to the label, I don't recall her ever not working," said L.A. Reid, chairman of the Island Def Jam Music Group. "I don't recall her ever taking time off for anything.... We've always had scheduling nightmares because this woman works so hard. She's absolutely one of the hardest-working artists I've ever met or been involved with at any level."

In fall 2007 Rihanna and Ne-Yo scored a hit together with their duet "Hate That I Love You," cowritten by Ne-Yo. The song relates the feeling of an overwhelming romantic relation-ship that leaves each partner feeling vulnerable. Reaching the top ten on the American pop charts, the song was also nominated for two Grammy Awards, as the best R&B perfor-mance by a duo or group and as the best R&B song of the year. The pair performed "Hate That I Love You" on the telecast of the American Music Awards in November 2007, where Ri-hanna was named Favorite Female Soul/R&B Artist of the year.

With hit after hit, *Good Girl Gone Bad* elevated Rihanna to a new level of global stardom in 2007 and enhanced her reputation as a singer who could delve into a broader range of subjects and genres. In a review of the album in *Entertainment Weekly*, Neil Drum-ming noted that "Rihanna's at her best when she's brash and unpre-dictable and summoning the spirit of years past." Zac Soto gave an enthu-siastic review in *Giant,* calling *Good Girl Gone Bad* "one of the most daring albums in the recent history of mainstream music. To say that this album exceeds expectations would be an understatement; it changes the way we should view Rihanna as an artist from now on."

Spokesperson for Beauty and Fitness Lines

With youth, beauty, charisma, and a global audience, Rihanna was quickly identified as a fashion trendsetter who would appeal to young consumers worldwide. By 2006 she had signed a number of product endorsement deals. Her image and music were used to promote tourism in Barbados and to market such well-known brands as Nike, JCPenney, Cover-Girl, and Fuzed. For the cosmetics line Clinique, Rihanna recorded "Just Be Happy," a jazzy, upbeat pop song to be used in promotion of the Happy fragrance. The Cov-erGirl campaign featured her in ads for lip products and included

A scene with Rihanna and Ne-Yo from the video for "Hate That I Love You."

life-size Rihanna stand-up cut outs in stores. Because she is young, she has maintained a special connection with teenaged fans. "I'm at the age where you start to cross over into young womanhood, but I'm still a teen and I love being a teen. I like to read magazines. I like to go shopping. I love using the telephone."

Rihanna has described herself as a "very fun-loving person" and a risk-taker. "I like to be adventurous in everything," she once said. "I like things that are cool. I hate the typical. I like to go bowling. I love going to the movies. That's just who I am." While her success in the music industry has transformed her life, as of 2007 she was still getting used to the idea of international celebrity. "Star-studded events kind of weird me out," she confided. "I'm scared to talk to anybody so I just stand in the corner!" She hopes to avoid the distractions that have landed some other young stars in jail or rehab and sees herself as a role model for other teens. "I'm very aware of the impact I have on people's lives … so I only wanna make positive ones. Why not help? Be that example they can follow. I always wanted to make a difference in the world. I was always trying to figure out how can I change the world."

Rihanna performing live on "The Today Show."

Rihanna remains humbled by the success she has achieved during her teen years. "It's definitely a fairytale, and I wake up every day so thankful," she revealed "It's just proof to everyone out there that no matter where you're from, if you work really hard and believe in your dreams they can come true."

HOME AND FAMILY

When she first traveled to the United States to work, Rihanna lived in Connecticut in the home of her music producer, Evan Rogers, and his wife, Jackie. In 2007 Rihanna moved into her own apartment in Los Angeles, California.

FAVORITE MUSIC

Rihanna lists the pop and R&B singers Mariah Carey, Whitney Houston, Brandy, and Beyoncé as particular influences. When recording *Good Girl Gone Bad*, she says, she listened to the Brandy album *Afrodisiac* and "admired that every song was a great song." Coming from the Caribbean, she also names several reggae artists among her influences: "Of course Bob Marley. I love Sean Paul. I love Beenie Man. Bounty Killer is still one of my favorites. Vybz Kartel. 'Redemption Song' is my all time favorite."

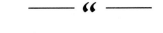

"It's definitely a fairytale, and I wake up every day so thankful," Rihanna revealed "It's just proof to everyone out there that no matter where you're from, if you work really hard and believe in your dreams they can come true."

HOBBIES AND OTHER INTERESTS

Rihanna founded the medical charity Believe, whose "goal is to assist children with life-threatening diseases," including AIDS, leukemia, and cancer, among others. An international organization, Believe raises money for medical research and funds medical care for those in need. In addition, Rihanna performed in a special benefit concert in May 2007 in New York City in support of the organ donation network DKMS and the Bone Marrow Association, and she also performed in the Live Earth concert in July 2007 in Tokyo, Japan.

SELECTED RECORDINGS

Music of the Sun, 2005
A Girl Like Me, 2006
Good Girl Gone Bad, 2007

SELECTED FILMS

Bring It On: All or Nothing, 2006

HONORS AND AWARDS

Billboard Music Awards: 2006 (three awards), Female Artist of the Year, Female Hot 100 Artist of the Year, Pop 100 Artist of the Year

MTV Video Awards: 2006, Best New Artist Video; 2007 (two awards; with Jay Z) Monster Single of the Year and Video of the Year, both for "Umbrella"

MuchMusic Video Awards: 2006, Best International Artist

Music of Black Origin (MOBO) Awards: 2006, Best R&B

Teen Choice Awards: 2006, Choice Music-R&B Artist; 2007, Choice Music-R&B Artist

American Music Awards: 2007, Favorite Soul/R&B Female Artist

World Music Awards: 2007, Female Entertainer of the Year

FURTHER READING

Periodicals

Billboard, Aug. 13, 2005; Mar. 18, 2006, p.18; Apr. 29, 2006, p.39; Apr. 28, 2007; p.36; May 12, 2007, p.24; June 9, 2007, p.63; June 16, 2007, p.36; Sep. 8, 2007, p.52

CosmoGirl, June/July 2007, p.53

Entertainment Weekly, May 19, 2006, p.29; June 8, 2007, p.79; June 29, 2007, p.80

Essence, June 2007, p.154

Giant, June/July 2007, p.76

Girls' Life, Aug. 1, 2006, p.40

Guardian (London), Nov. 25, 2005, p.9

Interview, Oct. 1, 2005, p.88

Jet, May 22, 2006, p.35; June 11, 2007, p.54

People, Aug. 29, 2005, p.49; Sep. 5, 2005, p.48

Teen Vogue, Nov. 2006, p.107

USA Today, Aug. 2, 2005, p.D3

Online Articles

http://www.eveningtimes.co.uk/timesout/display.var.1882868.0.music
_rihannas_fairytale_dreams_come_true.php
(Evening Times Scotland, "Rihanna's Fairy Tale Dreams Come True," Dec. 5, 2007)

http://www.giantmag.com/content.php?cid=135
(Giant, "Good Girl Gone Great," June 5, 2007)
http://www.mtv.com/news/articles/1535606/20060705/rihanna.jhtml?head
lines=true
(MTV.com, "Rihanna Lets Fans Be Her Guide, Selects Summer Jam 'We
Ride' as Next Single," June 6, 2006)
http://observer.guardian.co.uk/magazine/story/0,,2153857,00.html
(Observer/Guardian Online, "Singing in the Rain," Aug. 26, 2007)
http://www.rollingstone.com/artists/beyonce/articles/story/7567167
/rihanna_brings_riddims
(Rolling Stone, "Rihanna Brings Riddims," Aug. 18, 2005)

ADDRESS

Rihanna
Def Jam Recordings
825 Eighth Avenue
New York, NY 10019

WORLD WIDE WEB SITES

http://www.defjam.com
http://www.rihannanow.com
http://www.srprecords.com

John Roberts Jr. 1955-

American Lawyer
Chief Justice of the U.S. Supreme Court

BIRTH

John G. Roberts Jr. was born in Buffalo, New York, on January 27, 1955. His parents were John G. Roberts Sr., an executive with the Bethlehem Steel company, and Rosemary (Podrasky) Roberts, a homemaker. Roberts has three sisters, Kathy, Peggy, and Barbara.

YOUTH AND EDUCATION

Roberts spent most of his childhood in northwestern Indiana, where his family moved after his father accepted a job at a local steel plant. He grew up in Long Beach, a prosperous Indiana town not far from Chicago, Illinois. His childhood was a happy one, full of bike rides around the neighborhood and evening games of Monopoly and Scrabble with his sisters. Roberts also possessed a natural curiosity about the world around him that was nurtured by his parents. "We were very concerned about the news and everything," recalled his mother. "We have always been a family that was interested in things other than ourselves."

Roberts attended Catholic schools for both his elementary and high school education. He was self-motivated and smart, and he excelled in his studies. He did not just bury himself in books, however. During his four years at La Lumiere High School, an all-boys Catholic boarding school in La-Porte, Indiana, Roberts also immersed himself in a wide range of extracurricular activities. He wrestled, sang in the school choir, co-edited the school newspaper, served on the student council, and was chosen captain of the varsity football team his senior year. He even played the role of Peppermint Patty in an all-male school production of the musical *You're a Good Man, Charlie Brown.*

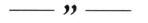

> "It became very, very clear and evident when he first came here," remembered one high school teacher, "that he was a person who was destined to do big things."

Despite his popularity and school spirit, though, Roberts remained best known for his intelligence, his maturity, and his conservative outlook on issues and events. When the administration at La Lumiere High School acknowledged that it was considering opening enrollment to girls, for example, Roberts promptly published an editorial in the school newspaper that strongly objected to the idea. "It became very, very clear and evident when he first came here," remembered one teacher in an interview with the *New York Times,* "that he was a person who was destined to do big things."

Attending Harvard

Roberts graduated first in his high school class of 25 students in 1973. He then enrolled at Harvard College, one of the most prestigious undergraduate schools in the world. He spent the next three academic years on the Harvard campus in Cambridge, Massachusetts, working on a history major. During each summer, though, he returned home to Indiana and worked at a steel mill to earn money for his tuition. "John was a serious student," recalled one of his roommates in an interview

The 1979 yearbook photo of the Harvard Law Review. *Roberts is in the third row from the front, the ninth person from the left.*

with the *Harvard Crimson.* "There were no parties, but John did have a social life."

Roberts earned a bachelor's degree in history *summa cum laude* (with highest honors) from Harvard College in 1976, finishing in only three years (instead of the usual four years). He then opted to continue his education at Harvard University Law School. A top student, he also found time to work as managing editor of the *Harvard Law Review,* a student-run journal that publishes articles on legal issues. It's a prestigious publication, and being one of its editors is a significant achievement. Roberts graduated *magna cum laude* (with high honors) from Harvard Law School in 1979.

Despite these accomplishments, Roberts was always modest about his intellectual abilities. "He was somebody who got along with everyone, who was obviously very bright but not aggressive," recalled a fellow editor in an interview with the *Harvard Crimson.* "He had a Midwestern reserve about not showing off how smart he was." Other college friends remembered him for his easygoing, friendly manner as well. "John and I probably spent several hundred hours debating every issue known to humankind, coming from very different perspectives on many issues," recalled one liberal Harvard classmate in the *New York Times.* "He's the type of person you could debate any issue with, and you could sometimes change his mind and sometimes he would change yours.... He was someone who's just soft-spoken and brilliant, but yet very interested in what other people had to say."

CAREER HIGHLIGHTS

After finishing law school, Roberts began a wide-ranging and impressive law career, working in many different types of legal positions. He started as a law clerk for Henry J. Friendly, one of the most influential and respected judges in the entire U.S. Court of Appeals. The federal judicial system, where Roberts clerked for Judge Friendly, is comprised of three different levels. The lower courts, the level at which most cases are originally tried, include 94 district courts. After a case is tried, the loser has the option of "appealing" the verdict (an appeal is a request to have a higher court hear the case in hopes that it will make a different ruling). Then the case would go to the next level, the court of appeals. There are 12 courts of appeals (also called circuit courts), organized geographically, that cover the 50 states and the District of Columbia. When a case is appealed, the appeals (or appellate) court judge reviews the lower court's decision and either sustains it (agrees) or overturns it (disagrees). After that step, the case could be taken to the Supreme Court, the highest court in the land and the final authority on American law. At all three levels in the U.S. judicial system, federal judges are nominated by the president, confirmed by the Senate, and serve for life.

> "He was somebody who got along with everyone, who was obviously very bright but not aggressive," recalled a fellow law student. "He had a Midwestern reserve about not showing off how smart he was."

As a law clerk for Judge Friendly, Roberts researched legal issues and also wrote judicial positions on the cases before the judge. After one year with Friendly, Roberts joined the staff of U.S. Supreme Court Justice William Rehnquist in 1980. He spent the next year as a law clerk for Rehnquist. In early 1981 he was named a special assistant to the Office of the U.S. Attorney General, which is responsible for overseeing the U.S. Department of Justice. Roberts spent the next year lending his legal expertise to the administration of Republican President Ronald Reagan. He reviewed presidential speeches, laws that had been proposed, and positions taken by the White House to make sure that they were legally sound.

Triumphs and Setbacks

In 1982 Roberts moved from the Department of Justice to the Office of White House Counsel. This office is an important one, for its staff serves as top advisors to the president of the United States on all legal issues concerning the White House. Roberts spent the next four years as an associate counsel. He then accepted a position at Hogan & Hartson, one of the most prestigious law firms in Washington DC, and worked there from 1986 to 1989. During this period he became known as one of the firm's most effective specialists in federal appellate law—the stage of the American legal process in which people, companies, or organizations unhappy with a trial verdict can appeal the verdict to an appeals court or to the U.S. Supreme Court.

In 1989 Roberts returned to governmental service, taking a position as principal deputy solicitor general with the U.S. Department of Justice. The solicitor general is the federal government's legal representative in all cases that come before the U.S. Supreme Court. This new job, then, gave Roberts lots of exposure to the Supreme Court and the individual justices who sat on the Court. On several occasions, he even argued cases before the Court.

In January 1992 Republican President George H.W. Bush nominated Roberts to fill a vacancy on the U.S. Court of Appeals for the Washington DC circuit. Roberts was extremely excited at the prospect of becoming a federal judge, but his nomination quickly became mired in politics. The U.S. Senate must confirm all federal judicial nominations, but the Democratic leadership of the Senate refused to bring his nomination up for a vote. The Democrats worried that his conservative view of the law would lead him to make rulings that ran counter to Democratic positions on civil rights, abortion rights, environmental protection, and other issues. The Democrats thus decided to block his nomination until the 1992 presidential election. They hoped that their party's presidential nominee, Bill Clinton, would win the upcoming election and replace Roberts with a nominee they considered more attractive.

The Democratic strategy worked. When Clinton defeated Bush to win the presidential election in November 1992, Roberts knew that his appeals court nomination was doomed. He refused to complain publicly about this setback, but friends and family members say that he was bitterly disappointed. Roberts returned to Hogan & Hartson in early 1993. He spent the next several years arguing dozens of cases before the U.S. Supreme

Court—and earning an annual salary of more than $1 million. In most of these cases, he represented "conservative" clients. On several occasions, though, he used his courtroom skills on behalf of "liberal" clients such as a group of environmentalists locked in a legal battle to preserve wilderness around Lake Tahoe—a famous outdoor destination on the California-Nevada border—and protect it from developers.

> "John and I probably spent several hundred hours debating every issue known to humankind, coming from very different perspectives on many issues," recalled one Harvard classmate. "He's the type of person you could debate any issue with, and you could sometimes change his mind and sometimes he would change yours.... He was someone who's just soft-spoken and brilliant, but yet very interested in what other people had to say."

A New President and a Nomination

In November 2000 Roberts became involved in the disputed presidential election between Democratic candidate Al Gore and Republican candidate George W. Bush (son of President George H.W. Bush). On election night, the vote count was so close that the winner of Florida would win the election and become president. But the vote count in Florida became a matter of tremendous controversy because of problems with ballot cards and voting machines.

In the days following the election, both campaigns mounted fierce legal efforts to place their candidate in the White House. During this legal battle, Roberts traveled to Florida to provide legal assistance to the Bush campaign. The Gore campaign turned to the U.S. court system to demand a recount of the Florida vote, and the issue quickly ended up in the U.S. Supreme Court. The conservative majority on the Supreme Court refused to approve the Gore campaign's demand for a recount, the Bush campaign prevailed, and George W. Bush became president.

A few months later, in early 2001, President Bush nominated Roberts to fill an open seat on the federal circuit court for Washington DC—the same seat for which he had been nominated eight years earlier by Bush's father, President George H.W. Bush. Once again, politics interfered with the nomination. Organizations devoted to preserving abortion rights were convinced that Roberts was hostile to their position, and they and other

President George W. Bush nominating Roberts for the Supreme Court. Roberts is accompanied by his family: (left to right) John, Jane, and Josephine.

progressive groups managed to convince their Senate allies to block his nomination for two years. In June 2003, however, his nomination finally came up for a vote. First his nomination was approved by the Senate Judiciary Committee by a 16-3 margin. This vote brought his nomination before the full Senate, which gave final approval to the nomination. A full decade after his first nomination, Roberts was finally a federal appeals court judge. He served in this capacity for the next two years.

Nominated to the U.S. Supreme Court

On July 19, 2005, Roberts once again returned to the public spotlight when President George W. Bush nominated him to fill a vacancy on the U.S. Supreme Court left by the retirement of Sandra Day O'Connor. "He has the qualities Americans expect in a judge: experience, wisdom, fairness, and civility," stated Bush in announcing his nomination.

Many Americans recognized that this nomination was an extremely important one for the future of the Supreme Court. Over the previous several years, the nine-member Court had been closely divided on a wide range of issues, including abortion. O'Connor had been the deciding fifth vote in favor of preserving abortion rights in several high-profile cases. Conservative and liberal observers alike believed that if she was replaced with a judge who opposed abortion rights, then legal access to abortion might be outlawed in the future.

Debate about Robert's nomination was fierce. On one side were pro-choice organizations and other liberal advocacy groups that disagreed with his conservative legal philosophy, and they urged the U.S. Senate to defeat his nomination. On the other side were opponents of abortion rights and other conservative voices, and they declared their support for his nomination. A *Wall Street Journal* editorial, for example, declared that his record as an appeals judge showed that Roberts would be a superb Supreme Court justice: "His opinions are meticulous and circumspect. He avoids sweeping pronouncements and bold strokes, and instead pays close attention to the legal material at hand. He is undoubtedly conservative. But ideology has played only a modest role in his judicial work."

———— `"` ————

"His opinions are meticulous and circumspect," declared a **Wall Street Journal** *editorial. "He avoids sweeping pronouncements and bold strokes, and instead pays close attention to the legal material at hand. He is undoubtedly conservative. But ideology has played only a modest role in his judicial work."*

———— `"` ————

In September 2005 the controversy surrounding Roberts took an unusual turn when Supreme Court Chief Justice William Rehnquist—for whom Roberts had clerked two decades earlier—died of thyroid cancer. Bush quickly withdrew Roberts's nomination for O'Connor's seat and instead recommended him to take Rehnquist's place as chief justice.

Becoming the Chief Justice of the Supreme Court

Senate Judiciary Committee hearings on the Roberts nomination opened on September 12, 2005, and continued for the next three days. During these hearings, many Democratic senators on the committee voiced concern about his record as a judge and as an attorney for two Republican administrations. They argued that the evidence showed that Roberts would be unfriendly to civil rights, voting rights, abortion rights, the separation of church and state, environmental protection, and other ideas that they supported. Republicans on the committee, meanwhile, praised him as a brilliant jurist who was dedicated to upholding basic constitutional principles.

Roberts being sworn in as Chief Justice of the U.S. Supreme Court by Justice John Paul Stevens, the senior justice on the court.

For his part, Roberts used his appearance before the committee to try to reassure doubters. "Judges and justices are servants of the law, not the other way around," he stated. "Judges are like umpires. Umpires don't make the rules; they apply them. The role of an umpire and a judge is critical. They make sure everybody plays by the rules. But it is a limited role. Nobody ever went to a ball game to see the umpire."

Roberts performed well throughout the hearings. Some Democratic senators voiced frustration with some of his answers, in which he avoided expressing personal views about abortion and other issues. But other Democrats expressed admiration for his legal mind, and Republicans were united in expressing support for his nomination. When the hearings concluded, his nomination was approved by the committee by a 13-5 vote. It was then approved by a 78-22 vote by the full Senate.

Roberts was sworn in as the 17th chief justice of the U.S. Supreme Court on September 29, 2005. He was sworn in by Justice John Paul Stevens, the most senior justice on the Supreme Court. Roberts thus became the first justice to join the Court in more than 11 years—the longest stretch with-out a new member since 1823. He also became the youngest chief jus-tice—50 years old—since his idol John Marshall took the same role in 1801 at the age of 45. Four months later, Samuel Alito replaced O'Connor to bring the Court up to its full nine members.

The Role of the Supreme Court

As chief justice, Roberts presides over America's judicial branch, one of the three branches of the U.S. government. The other two branches are the leg-islative branch (Congress) and the executive branch (the Presidency). Each of these branches has clearly defined responsibilities. The legislative branch makes laws, the executive branch car-ries out laws, and the judicial branch interprets the laws, making sure that they do not violate the U.S. Constitu-tion. The U.S. Supreme Court is the ultimate authority on American law; once the Supreme Court rules on a case, the decision is final.

> ———— " ————
>
> *"Judges and justices are servants of the law, not the other way around," Roberts stated. "Judges are like umpires. Umpires don't make the rules; they apply them. The role of an umpire and a judge is critical. They make sure everybody plays by the rules. But it is a limited role. Nobody ever went to a ball game to see the umpire."*
>
> ———— " ————

In joining the Supreme Court, Roberts became one of nine judges—one chief justice and eight associate jus-tices—on the highest court in the country. The Supreme Court decides whether the laws made by all levels of government—federal, state, and local—follow the Constitution. The Court accomplishes this by interpret-ing the provisions of the Constitution and applying its rules to specific legal cases. Because the Constitution lays out general rules, the Court tries to determine their meaning and figure out how to apply them to modern sit-uations. After the justices select a case for review—and they accept fewer than about 100 of the 6,000 cases presented to them each year—they first will hear arguments by the two opposing sides. They begin discussing the case, take a preliminary vote, and then one justice from the majority is as-signed to write up the Court's opinion. Drafting an opinion is complex and time-consuming, and the whole process can take over a year. The Court's final opinion has tremendous importance, setting out a precedent that all lower courts and all levels of government throughout the United States are required to follow. The reasoning given in the opinion is also important, because it helps people understand the basis for the decision and how the ruling might apply to other cases in the future.

As Roberts shouldered the challenge of leading the Court, many people expressed confidence in his abilities. Justice Stevens, perhaps the most liberal member of the Court, publicly declared that he already had the trust of the other justices. Sandra Day O'Connor also spoke in glowing terms about his capacity to lead the Court. "As Justice Byron White used to say, the arrival of a new justice creates an entirely new court," she wrote in *Time* magazine in early 2006. "This is particularly true when the new justice is also the new chief justice. The new chief can bring tremendous changes in the operations of the court, from the way cases are discussed and opinions written to the very guiding ethos and atmosphere. Few have made the transition as seamlessly and effectively as Roberts. He knew our traditions well, as he had clerked in 1980 for then Associate Justice Rehnquist. His sense of humor and articulate nature and calm demeanor combine to make him a very effective chief. I'm certain he will serve a long tenure in the role and be an effective leader not only for the Supreme Court but for all the federal courts in the nation."

For his part, Roberts spoke about the need to seek common ground among the members of the Court. In 2006 he asserted that "working toward broader agreement should be one of the shared aims" of all Court justices, and in 2007 he stated that "the Court functions most effectively as a judicial institution saying what the law is when it can deliver one clear and focused opinion of the Court." As time passed, however, Roberts frequently found himself presiding over a bitterly divided Court.

Areas of Unity and Division

During the first two Supreme Court terms with Roberts as chief justice, he has achieved mixed results in efforts to unify the Court on legal issues facing the nation. On the one hand, legal observers point out that under his leadership, the percentage of unanimous Supreme Court decisions in 2006 and 2007 was actually higher than it had been in the final years of the Rehnquist-led Court. The Roberts Court also had a lower percentage of total cases decided by a 5-4 vote. A writer for the conservative *Weekly Standard* applauded these trends and proposed that "over time, the Roberts effect may produce not only larger majorities and more stable rulings but also a Court that ... pays more attention to working out the relevant law and less to mere politics.... The prospect of the continuing advancement of that philosophy is a happy one, and a reason to say hail to this particular chief."

As Chief Justice, Roberts has tried to unite the Supreme Court, shown here in 2006.

Roberts told *Atlantic Monthly* that his previous career experiences have helped him enormously as chief justice. "I do think it's extremely valuable for people to be on both sides, and I mean being in private practice and being in government, arguing against the government and for the government. It does give you a perspective that you just can't get any other way, in terms of what the concerns of the other side are. And it also gives you an added credibility, and that's very, very important."

Other Court watchers, though, have pointed out that Roberts's own voting record since joining the Supreme Court is a very conservative one. They also claim that the addition of Roberts and Alito has swung the balance of power on the Court toward conservatives in a number of major policy areas. These observers note that by 5-4 votes, the Supreme Court in 2006-07 issued rulings that weakened abortion rights, struck down campaign finance laws, and limited the ability of school boards to adopt voluntary desegregation plans that use race as a factor in enrollment. All of these rulings, which reversed earlier legal precedents, were hailed by conservatives and condemned by liberals.

In some of these cases, the liberal justices on the Supreme Court have voiced clear anger with Roberts and his conservative allies on the bench. These justices have issued a string of harshly worded dissents. Justice Stephen Breyer, a liberal, even declared that in the entire history of the United States, rarely have "so few so quickly changed so much" in American law.

Roberts has been critical of the media coverage of the Supreme Court. He has acknowledged that the members of the Court have disagreed strongly on several important cases and that the liberal justices have become frustrated in some instances. But he also expressed his belief that media coverage of the Court has not paid enough attention to the large number of unanimous decisions that the justices have handed down since he came on board. He also pointed out in a 2007 interview with *Atlantic Monthly* that "a chief justice has the same vote that everyone else has.... [His] authority is really quite limited, and the dynamic among all the justices is going to affect whether he can accomplish much or not."

In July 2007 Roberts suffered a seizure while vacationing in Maine. This seizure, which was similar to one that he experienced in 1993, led doctors to wonder whether he might have a mild form of epilepsy. Epilepsy is a physical disorder in which the electrical activity of the brain is interrupted for brief periods of time. In severe cases, this interruption can result in loss of consciousness or uncontrolled muscle spasms. Roberts was released after a brief hospital stay, and reporters openly wondered whether doctors might put him on medication to prevent future seizures. Even if Roberts is formally diagnosed with epilepsy, however, the disorder is not expected to interfere with his duties as chief justice.

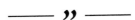

"Few have made the transition as seamlessly and effectively as Roberts," said Associate Justice Sandra Day O'Connor. "His sense of humor and articulate nature and calm demeanor combine to make him a very effective chief. I'm certain he will serve a long tenure in the role and be an effective leader not only for the Supreme Court but for all the federal courts in the nation."

MARRIAGE AND FAMILY

Roberts married Jane Marie Sullivan, a fellow lawyer, in 1996. They live in the wealthy suburb of Chevy Chase, Maryland, outside Washington DC. They have two children, Josephine and John.

HOBBIES AND OTHER INTERESTS

Roberts enjoys playing golf and listening to the opera. He also enjoys reading and playing with his young children.

FURTHER READING

Books

McElroy, Lisa Tucker. *John Roberts Jr.: Chief Justice,* 2006 (juvenile)
Toobin, Jeffrey. *The Nine: Inside the Secret World of the Supreme Court,* 2007

Periodicals

Atlantic Monthly, Jan./Feb. 2007, p.110
Current Biography Yearbook, 2006
Economist, July 23, 2005; Sep. 10, 2005
New York Times, July 21, 2005, p.A1; June 28, 2007, p.A1; Aug. 1, 2007, p.A1
New Yorker, June 25, 2007, p.35
Newsweek, Aug. 1, 2005, p.22; Aug. 15, 2005, p.23; Jan. 30, 2006, p.68; Mar. 6, 2006, p.44
People, Sep. 12, 2005, p.109
Time, Aug. 1, 2005, p.30; Sep. 5, 2005, p.28; Apr. 30, 2006; July 10, 2006, p.26; Feb. 26, 2007, p.44; Oct. 22, 2007, p.40
U.S. News and World Report, Oct. 1, 2007
USA Today, Aug. 31, 2005, p.A13; Dec. 28, 2005, p.A4; June 26, 2006, p.A4; July 6, 2006, p.A11; Apr. 10, 2007, p.A1; June 29, 2007, p.A8
Washington Post, Sep. 14, 2005, p.A1; Sep. 30, 2005, p.A1
Weekly Standard, Mar. 20, 2006

Online Articles

http://supreme.lp/findlaw.com/supreme_court/justices/roberts.html
   (FindLaw Online, "John G. Roberts," undated)
http://www.thecrimson.com/article.aspx?ref=508284
   (Harvard Crimson Online, "Alum Picked as Court Nominee," July 22, 2005)

ADDRESS

John Roberts
U.S. Supreme Court
Supreme Court Bldg.
1 First Street NE
Washington, DC 20543

WORLD WIDE WEB SITES

http://www.oyez.org
http://www.supremecourtus.gov
http://www.uscourts.gov/index.html

James Stewart Jr. 1985-

American Motorcycle Racer
2007 AMA Supercross Series Champion

BIRTH

James Stewart Jr., known to race fans as "Bubba," was born on December 21, 1985, in Bartow, Florida. His father, James Sr., worked as a supervisor at a Coca-Cola bottling plant before becoming his son's full-time riding coach. His mother, Sonya, also helps manage their son's business affairs. James Jr. has one younger brother, Malcolm.

YOUTH

Ever since he was a toddler, Stewart has been passionate about motorcycles. He loved going to local dirt tracks to watch his father, who was an amateur rider. Before long, he was constantly badgering his parents for his own little motorbike. "Little James, he wanted to ride from the time he was in diapers," his mother recalled. "We'd come home from work and Little James would just beg us to take him riding. We'd say, 'We're tired!' but he was like, 'I want to go!' So if he wants to do it, you continue to do it. And that's what made him better."

According to Stewart, racing appealed to his competitive nature. "In school I raced kids [during tests] to finish first," he said. "I slammed the pencil down so that everybody knew I was done. 'Done!'" His love for motorbike racing, though, was so great that other competitive sports never really interested him. "I never played much football or baseball," Stewart admitted. "I just wanted to be a bike racer."

> *Stewart's love for motorbike racing was so great that other competitive sports never really interested him. "I never played much football or baseball," he admitted. "I just wanted to be a bike racer."*

"Boogie," as he was known within his family, started racing 50cc (cubic centimeters) motorbikes at age four. He won his first national junior AMA (American Motorcycle Association) title when he was seven years old. (These events are officially called amateur events, but junior is the term by which they're usually known.) As he grew older, he also frequently went with his father to professional AMA events. These weekends exposed him to the best riders in both supercross and motocross, which are the two main types of competitive dirt-track motorcycle racing in the United States. Supercross races are held inside arenas and stadiums from January through May, taking place on shorter but more treacherous man-made dirt tracks. Motocross races are held outdoors from May through September, taking place on outdoor dirt tracks on natural terrain. For both, the riders participate in events over the course of the season, and the winner is determined by the number of wins during the season.

During race weekends, it was not unusual for Stewart and members of his family to be the only African Americans in attendance. According to Stewart, skin color was never an issue for him or other riders. "When I came in it I was such a young kid. I was so small and so young, I never really

Stewart in his garage on his family's farm in Haines City, Florida, showing off some of his motorcycles. The family gradually built up the property with a practice track, outdoor lighting for night riding, a motorcycle garage that holds Stewart's three dozen motorcycles, and multiple buildings for the family's fleet of vehicles.

thought about it," he explained. "And then once I realized everything—oh, there's not a lot of 'me' out there—I was already used to it."

EARLY INFLUENCES

Stewart credits his father's guidance and racing smarts for his early success. "My dad has had more of an impact in my career than anyone could ever imagine," he declared. "He has always pushed me and saw things in me that I didn't know I had. He helped me pull things out such as heart, courage, and a strong mind."

Stewart's mother also played an important role in his racing career. "My mom's the backbone of the family," he explained. "My dad comes to the races with me on the weekend, and my mom's back doing the tickets, going to the races with my brother, making dinner and stuff like that. She's keeping us in line."

Another important influence in Stewart's young life was Tony Haynes, who was one of the few other junior African-American motocross riders in America when Stewart was growing up. Stewart and his father even shared quarters with Haynes and his father when the two young riders were competing at the same track on racing weekends. In 1992, however, Haynes suffered a terrible crash on the track that left him paralyzed from the waist down. A short time later, Stewart asked his injured friend if he could wear the number 259—Haynes's number—in future competitions. Touched by Stewart's efforts to pay tribute to him, Haynes agreed. Stewart wore the number 259 jersey for the next 13 years, and he and Haynes remain close friends.

> "
>
> *"My dad has had more of an impact in my career than anyone could ever imagine,"* Stewart declared. *"He has always pushed me and saw things in me that I didn't know I had. He helped me pull things out such as heart, courage, and a strong mind."*
>
> "

Riding with the number 259 on his back, Stewart spent the rest of the 1990s building a legendary reputation in the world of junior motorcycle racing. He became the rider to beat in every age category through which he passed, but few competitors were able to challenge him.

Stewart's dominance became even greater after 1998, when his family moved to a 40-acre parcel of land in Haines City, Florida, and built a practice dirtbike track for him. The young racing wizard spent hours on the track every day, honing his skills and practicing new moves to shave valuable seconds off his time. By 2001 "Bubba" Stewart, as he was known throughout the sport, had recorded an amazing 47 race victories in junior AMA competition and 11 AMA national junior titles.

EDUCATION

Stewart attended public school in Florida until middle school, when his race schedule became so demanding that his parents decided to home-school him. Stewart has acknowledged that he missed out on some of the pleasures of traditional school experiences. "I kind of wish I went to a prom," he once said. "Sometimes, it bums me out when people go: 'I got Homecoming this weekend; I'm taking so-and-so.'" Ultimately, however, Stewart believes that his decision to focus on his racing career was the correct one.

CAREER HIGHLIGHTS

In 2001, after years on the junior circuit, the 16-year-old Stewart made the leap to professional motorcycle racing. He started out in the 125 class, the

Stewart made this jump in 2002, while still a rookie.

lower class or level of professional motocross and supercross. The name comes from the 125cc bikes used by riders in the lower class at that time. In the early 2000s, though, the class transitioned to more powerful 250cc four-stroke models, and in 2005 the division formally changed its name to Lites Class. As it turned out, it did not matter what sort of motorcycle Stewart rode. He dominated the field in race after race throughout his four years in the Lites Class, earning Lites Motocross Championship titles in both 2002 and 2004.

As usual, Stewart was often the only African-American rider in the field. But he never let this fact become a distraction. "Sometimes it's hard, when you look around and don't see any other African Americans racing," he admitted. "But you have more [African Americans] coming to the races to watch and if I'm bringing them in, that's cool. It does feel good to be the first ever, but I honestly don't sit here and think about it a lot. With a helmet on, we all look the same anyway."

> "Sometimes it's hard, when you look around and don't see any other African Americans racing," Stewart admitted. "But you have more [African Americans] coming to the races to watch and if I'm bringing them in, that's cool. It does feel good to be the first ever, but I honestly don't sit here and think about it a lot. With a helmet on, we all look the same anyway."

Stewart preferred to focus his attention on the sheer thrill of riding. Whether soaring airborne over hills, tearing down beaten-up straightaways, or flying through hairpin turns, the young star enjoyed every minute of every race. "It's kind of like the same feeling you get on a roller coaster ride!" he said.

During this period, Stewart became particularly famous for a riding stunt known as the Bubba Scrub, in which he tilts his motorcycle sideways in midair on steep jumps so that he can return to the ground sooner than other riders. "It's mind-boggling to see it," one racing journalist told *Sports Illustrated.* "He's doing things on a motorcycle that other people haven't considered."

Achieving Fame

By 2004 Stewart was earning more than $3 million a year in prize money and endorsements from such companies as Kawasaki (his motorcycle sponsor) and Oakley sunglasses. These earnings enabled the Stewart family to make major investments in their Haines City property, from building a new motorcycle garage to installing a bank of towering field lights along the practice track so that Stewart and his friends could ride at night. Stewart and his father also used the earnings to indulge their love of four-wheeled vehicles. By 2004 the family had a fleet of trucks, SUVs, and vintage cars tucked away in the various buildings on their property.

During this same period, Stewart became so famous that such professional sports stars as baseball players Barry Larkin and Ken Griffey Jr. regularly dropped in to ride with him. Both Larkin and Griffey bought several motorcycles for their families and kept them at the Stewart home. Stewart also became friendly with basketball legend Michael Jordan. "He was the first person I was ever nervous to meet," he admitted. "Now I talk to him all the time."

Stewart's racing exploits also led to interest from major media magazines and newspapers. He was featured in stories in *Sports Illustrated, Rolling Stone,* the *Washington Post, USA Today,* and the *New York Times.* In 2003 *Teen People* even named him as one of 20 teens "who will change the world." Despite all this attention, though, Stewart has said that he is just an ordinary guy who likes to race motorcycles. "I may have cars and money now, but I'm the same person I was before," he said. "If I worked at McDonald's, I'd be the same person."

Joining the Heavyweights

In January 2005 Stewart made his long-awaited move up into the premier class, the highest class of professional dirt-bike racing. By moving up into the supercross and motocross field, he would be riding bigger and more powerful 450cc motorbikes. He would also be competing against top riders like Ricky Carmichael, who had been the king of professional motorcycle racing for several years. "It's more pressure now," Stewart said. "People expect me to win. There are greater expectations, and my job is to make sure people believe."

Motorcycling fans all across America were thrilled at the prospect of watching a season's worth of showdowns between Stewart and Carmichael. But Stewart broke his arm during a practice session before the second race of the 2005 supercross season (which runs from January through May). He missed nearly half of the season before he was able to return to competition. When he did climb back aboard his Kawasaki, though, he showed that he would be a force to be reckoned with. In his second race after his return, at a supercross event in Dallas, Stewart led all

*Stewart leading Travis Pastrana during a round of the
2006 AMA Supercross Series.*

20 laps of the final and crossed under the checkered flag five seconds before Carmichael. "I'm so happy," he said afterward. "I have one [Supercross victory] under my belt, and now I know how it feels."

Stewart finished his rookie year in supercross with three victories and managed to climb to tenth place in the season-ending standings. He then turned his attention to the upcoming outdoor motocross season (which runs from May through September). Unfortunately, a serious bacterial infection bothered him for much of the outdoor season, and he was unable to make a major impact. "You have to learn to deal with the positives and the negatives," he later said. "I think champions are built when they overcome adversity and shine even better the next time. Some of the races I lost, I felt like I came back stronger the next weekend."

Winning the Championship

In 2006 Stewart retired his legendary 259 jersey and started wearing the number 7. He explained that he had taken the 259 number to the top of the Lites world, but that he was ready for a change as he set out on the next phase of his career. As the 2006 campaign unfolded, Stewart proved that he had put the injuries and illness that marred his rookie year behind him. In the AMA Supercross Series, he raced to eight wins and finished second in the year-end standings. he posted another three victories in the AMA Motocross Championship, which lifted him to fourth place in the final standings.

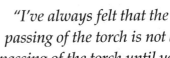

"I've always felt that the passing of the torch is not a passing of the torch until you earn it. Now I feel like I've earned [the reputation as the country's top rider]. A lot of people were trying to hand it to me before I won a championship, and that's not for me."

In 2007 Stewart finally claimed the ultimate championship of his sport. He utterly dominated the year's supercross circuit, winning 13 of the 16 races in which he competed. "It feels great," he declared. "I've always felt that the passing of the torch is not a passing of the torch until you earn it. Now I feel like I've earned [the reputation as the country's top rider]. A lot of people were trying to hand it to me before I won a championship, and that's not for me." His favorite race of the season was one that took place in Indianapolis, when he rocketed from far back in the pack to win the 20-lap final. "That might be one of the best races of my career," he said. "Like an NFL team in the Super Bowl, I was pulling out every trick play in the book to win that one."

By capturing the 2007 AMA Supercross Championship in the 450cc Division, Stewart became the first ever African-American AMA champion. As the 2007 motocross season got underway, he was poised to claim that championship as well. He was the season's points leader as the riders headed into Washougal, Washington, in late July for the eighth race in the season's 12-race schedule. But Stewart injured his knee in Washougal and was forced to sit out the rest of the season, so he slid to seventh in the final standings. "I was bummed because I love racing for my fans and I wanted to win that other title," he said. "[But] it gave me a well-needed break. I haven't had a break since the 2005 season. I have been grinding it out a long time and I think it's good to give my body a break and a chance to heal up. It gets me really motivated for the upcoming season. When you keep racing all the time it starts to get old but now it's like a slap in the face which really motivates me."

> "
>
> *Motorcycle racing legend Jeremy McGrath claimed that "Stewart can do things on a bike that nobody ever has.... He is a student, he watches tapes of myself and other people, and he has taken his skills one step further. He sees the little things, the things an average fan, even an average rider, might not see. Just amazing."*
>
> "

Entering the 2008 season, no one in the world of professional dirt-bike racing doubts that Stewart is the best rider in the sport. "I don't think anyone is on his level right now," said Carmichael. "There really is no one in his league." Another motorcycle racing legend, Jeremy McGrath, claimed that "Stewart can do things on a bike that nobody ever has.... He is a student, he watches tapes of myself and other people, and he has taken his skills one step further. He sees the little things, the things an average fan, even an average rider, might not see. Just amazing."

HOME AND FAMILY

Stewart lives and practices at his family's compound in Haines City, Florida. One of the buildings on the property houses the three dozen or so motorcycles that Stewart has ridden over the years, from the little 50cc bikes he rode as a youngster to the monster 450cc Kawasaki models he races today. Another building contains the hundreds of trophies that he has

Stewart winning his 13th race of 2007 in this season finale in Las Vegas, where he clinched the 2007 AMA National Supercross Championship.

earned over the years. "I have to put them out there because I don't have enough room in the house," said his mother. "It's crazy!"

HOBBIES AND OTHER INTERESTS

Stewart enjoys relaxing with music and video games in his spare time.

HONORS AND AWARDS

AMA Amateur National Championship: 11 titles from 1993-2001
AMA Rookie of the Year: 2002
AMA Lites National Motocross Championship: 2002, 2004
AMA Lites West Supercross Championship: 2003
AMA Lites East Supercross Championship: 2004
AMA National Supercross Championship: 2007

FURTHER READING

Books

Amick, Bill. *Motocross America*, 2005
Savage, Jeff. *James Stewart*, 2007 (juvenile)

Periodicals

Cincinnati Post, Apr. 13, 2002, p.B2
Detroit Free Press, Apr. 2, 2004, p.H4
Detroit News, Apr. 20, 2007, p.E8
Hartford (CT) Courant, June 7, 2002, p.A1
Los Angeles Times, Jan. 8, 2005, p.D1
Orlando Sentinel, Mar. 8, 2003, p.E1
Sacramento (CA) Observer, May 19, 2004, p.3
San Jose (CA) Mercury News, Jan. 28, 2006, p.3
Sports Illustrated, Apr. 29, 2002, p.A35; Apr. 11, 2005, p.Z8
Sports Illustrated for Kids, Mar. 2004, p.34; July 2007, p.36
St. Petersburg (FL) Times, Dec. 18, 2004, p.C1
USA Today, Apr. 30, 2003, p.C6; Nov. 30, 2005, p.C2; May 4, 2007, p.C7
Washington Post, July 23, 2004, p.A1

Online Articles

http://www.dirtbikemagazine.com
    (Dirt Rag Magazine, "James Stewart: The Future of MX," Nov. 9, 2000)

ADDRESS

James Stewart
Kawasaki Motors Corp., USA
9950 Jeronimo Road
Irvine, CA 92618

WORLD WIDE WEB SITES

http://www.jamesstewartonline.com
http://www.amamotocross.com
http://www.kawasaki.com
http://www.racerxill.com
http://www.supercrossonline.com
http://www.amaproracing.com

Ichiro Suzuki 1973-

Japanese Professional Baseball Player with the
Seattle Mariners
First Japanese Position Player in American Major
League Baseball

BIRTH

Ichiro Suzuki (pronounced *EE-chee-row suh-ZOO-ki*) was born
on October 22, 1973, in Kasugai, a city in the Aichi prefecture
(a regional government) of Japan. The name "Ichiro" is generally given to the first son in a family, but Ichiro was the second
son of Nobuyuki Suzuki, a businessman who owned a me-
chanical parts plant, and his wife Yoshie. Ichiro's older brother,

Kazuyasu Suzuki, is a fashion designer in Japan who specializes in hip-hop style clothing.

YOUTH

Suzuki grew up in Nagoya, the capital of the Aichi prefecture, a city located about 160 miles from Tokyo, the Japanese capital. Baseball has always been part of his life, and one of his earliest memories involved receiving a bat and glove at age three. "The glove wasn't a toy, but a real glove made of red leather," he recalled. "I was so excited about getting it I carried it everywhere." Suzuki's father was a big baseball fan who played the sport in high school. He also coached the local little league team, which young Ichiro convinced him to let him join at age six, two years early. Because the team only practiced on Sundays, his father helped him practice hitting and catching during the week. After work, the elder Suzuki devoted time every day to helping young Ichiro improve his game. He would also take his son to games played by Nagoya's home team, the Chinuchi Dragons of the Central League.

His father was very strict in training Ichiro, forbidding junk food and limiting television time. "Sometimes it was pretty hard to take," the athlete recalled. "It bordered on hazing. I suffered a lot." Still, he admitted, "once I started training again I'd enjoy it," and all the practice paid off. The naturally right-handed Ichiro learned to bat left-handed, bringing him a couple steps closer to first base. He became so skilled at hitting that by the time he was 10, his father's pitches didn't provide enough of a challenge. They would go to a local batting center, where Ichiro would hit 60-mile-an-hour pitches, as many as 250 every night. By the time Suzuki reached junior high, the center had to install a special spring on the batting machine so that it would shoot out 80-mile-an-hour pitches. His pitching arm was also outstanding, and he helped his junior high team place third in a national tournament.

EDUCATION

Suzuki was a good student in junior high, earning A's and B's. After taking his high school entrance exams, he enrolled in the Aiko-dai Meiden High School in Nagoya, a school that had a rich baseball tradition. It was too far for him to commute, so he stayed in a dormitory on campus and worked hard on his training. Suzuki became a standout pitcher for the Aiko-dai team, with a 93-mph fastball. After a bike accident left him on crutches for six weeks, he lost some of his pitching form and began to focus more on fielding and batting.

During Suzuki's sophomore and junior years, his team qualified to attend the Koshien, Japan's National High School Baseball Tournament. Only 50 of more than 3,000 high school baseball teams qualify each year. Unfortunately, Suzuki's team lost in the first round each time. His team failed to qualify for the Koshien during his senior year, but his performance in the regional tournament—batting .643—made professional scouts take notice. He graduated from high school in 1991 and entered the draft for Nippon Professional Baseball (NPB). Selected in the fourth round by the Orix Blue Wave, he decided to begin his professional baseball career rather than attend college. Suzuki believed baseball was his future. "If I wasn't going to be a ballplayer, I [couldn't] think of anything else."

CAREER HIGHLIGHTS

Beginning His Pro Career in Japan

Suzuki signed a contract with the Orix Blue Wave, which played in the port city of Kobe, 100 miles away from his hometown. His team didn't expect much of him at first. At 5'9" and only 150 pounds, he was considered too small to handle the demands of being a major league pitcher. Instead, his fielding and hitting skills gave him potential as an outfielder. He began playing in 1992 with Orix's minor league affiliate, and in 58 games he batted .366 and led the minors in stolen bases.

———— " ————

One of Suzuki's earliest memories involved receiving a bat and glove at age three. "The glove wasn't a toy, but a real glove made of red leather," he recalled. "I was so excited about getting it I carried it everywhere."

———— " ————

Called up to the Blue Wave for their final 40 games of the season, Suzuki hit a respectable .253. He began the 1993 season back down in the minors, where he hit a blistering .371. When he returned to the Blue Wave, however, the manager tried to force him to change his unconventional batting stance. At the time, Suzuki kicked up his front leg before hitting the ball, using its downward motion to add to his swing's power. Under pressure to change his stance, the outfielder hit only .188 during his 43 major-league games in 1993. During those first two partial seasons in the majors, however, he didn't make a single error in the outfield.

Suzuki's luck turned in 1994, when Orix changed managers. Akira Ohgi had seen the outfielder play in a winter league in Hawaii, where his .311 batting average helped his team win the league. Ohgi was willing to let him keep his unconventional batting style, as long as he worked hard and

Baseball in Japan

Baseball was introduced to Japan in about 1872 by Horace Wilson, a Civil War veteran from Maine. Wilson was teaching at the Kaisei Gakko School in Tokyo when he decided his students needed a break from studying. The students were intrigued by this simple game involving hitting a ball with a stick, throwing, catching, and running. They called it *yakyu,* or "field ball." As the sport grew in popularity throughout the country, the first organized team formed around 1883 and the game spread to high school and college campuses throughout Japan. A national high school baseball tournament, the Koshien, was founded in 1915. Today, the Koshien is one of Japan's most popular sporting events.

The first Japanese professional baseball team, the Shibaura Club, appeared in the early 1920s, but the sport didn't take off until seven teams created the Japan Baseball League in 1936. These teams were founded by newspaper and train companies that hoped to boost sales. The teams were named after their companies, not their home cities, a tradition that continues today. During Japan's involvement in World War II, between 1940 and 1945, many baseball teams ceased playing or even dissolved. After Japan's surrender to the United States in 1945, however, the sport returned. American soldiers helped the Japanese rebuild playing fields, and in 1950 the Japan Baseball League reorganized into Nippon Professional Baseball (NPB).

The NPB structure includes 12 teams split into two leagues. The Central League consists of the Chunichi Dragons, the Hanshin Tigers, the Hiroshima Carp, the Yakult Swallows, the Yokohama Bay Stars, and the Yomiuri Giants. The Pacific League consists of the Chiba Lotte Marines, the Nippon Ham Fighters, the Orix Buffaloes (formerly the Blue Wave, Ichiro Suzuki's team), the Rakuten Golden Eagles, the Seibu Lions, and the Softbank Hawks. After a season, which lasts between 130 and 140 games, the two league champions meet in the Japan Series. Japanese professional baseball has most of the same rules as American baseball, except that games can end in a tie after 12 innings. Japanese teams also put much less emphasis on home runs than do American teams.

Some observers have wondered whether the NPB will suffer now that many of their biggest stars have left to play in America, but Suzuki has suggested that "the more that Japanese players go to the big leagues to play and succeed, the more that will serve to inspire young kids in Japan to want to become baseball players." With more potential players, plus Japanese major leaguers bringing their skills back to Japan, he added, "in the long run, it will be a plus."

supported the team. He put Suzuki on his roster for the beginning of the season and made a unique suggestion: that his outfielder use his first name on his jersey instead of "Suzuki," which is one of the most common surnames in Japan. Suzuki resisted at first—no other player had ever gone by his first name—but Ohgi insisted it would bring good luck. Thus "Ichiro" debuted in the Orix outfield in the spring of 1994.

It didn't take long for Japanese baseball fans to take notice of Ichiro. During the first 17 games of the season, he hit nearly .400 with four home runs. His hitting streak of 69 games between May and August set a Japanese record. The Blue Wave was in the pennant race for most of the season, while fans all over the country watched Suzuki chase the 200-hit mark, a number no Japanese player had ever reached. He ended the 130-game season with 210 hits, a .385 batting average, and 29 stolen bases. He earned a Gold Glove for fielding and was named to the Best Nine, Japan's equivalent of the All-Star Team. He topped it off by being named the Pacific League's Most Valuable Player, even though his team finished second in the league.

The 1995 season began under a dark cloud for the Orix Blue Wave. On January 17, their home city of Kobe had been hit by a major earthquake that measured 7.2 on the Richter scale. More than 6,300 people died, and more than 7,000 buildings were damaged or destroyed. As the baseball season started, there were city-wide efforts to rebuild and boost morale, and the Blue Wave became part of that effort. Suzuki was inspired that Kobe fans continued to come out for games. "They'd gone through much and you'd think baseball wasn't much of a priority, but they still came to cheer us on," he commented. "That encouraged us a lot, and we did our best to live up to their expectations." That year he led the league in batting average (.358), RBIs (80), hits (179), and stolen bases (49), helping his team win the Pacific League pennant. Although the Blue Wave lost the Japan Series, Suzuki earned another Gold Glove, Best Nine, and MVP award.

Suzuki had another standout year in 1996. He led the Pacific League with a .356 batting average and 193 hits on the way to a third consecutive MVP citation. He also earned Gold Glove and Best Nine citations. Even better, the Blue Wave won the Pacific League pennant. In the Japan Series, they faced the Yomiuri Giants, Japan's most successful franchise, which had 18 previous Japan Series titles. The first game went into extra innings when the teams were tied 3-3 after the first nine. In the tenth inning, Suzuki hit a homer off pitcher Hirofumi Kono to score the winning run. The Blue Wave went on to win the Series four games to one.

Suzuki blasting a homer to score the winning run against the Yomiuri Giants in October 1996. The game went into extra innings when the teams were tied at the bottom of the 9th. With Suzuki's home run in the 10th inning, the Blue Wave won the first game of the 1996 Japan Series and went on to win the Series 4-1.

Becoming a Japanese Superstar

Suzuki's success with the Orix Blue Wave made him an extremely popular figure in Japan. Reporters began following his every move and fans crowded him in public, even in public restrooms. He was known by a single name—Ichiro—and one survey showed he was more famous than the Japanese emperor. For a young man still in his early 20s, this kind of attention was head-turning. "I was flattered and I wanted to see what they were saying about me, to read it every day," he admitted. "But I realized I should not have those kinds of feelings. It showed there was something wrong inside me." He turned back to baseball and focused on improving his skills. He had a new ambition: to play in the American major leagues. In late 1996 a team of American All-Stars had come to Japan, and Suzuki had performed well against them, getting seven hits in 11 at-bats during eight exhibition games. "I saw these good American players and I wanted to play against them," he recalled. Unfortunately, his contract tied him to the Orix Blue Wave through the 2001 season, and the team would not release its star player, who drew thousands of fans to the stadium.

Suzuki didn't let his disappointment affect his play. In 1997 he had another stellar season, leading the league with 185 hits and a .345 batting average. He also set a Japanese record with 216 consecutive at-bats without a strikeout. He earned a fourth consecutive Gold Glove, committing only two errors in 135 games, and another Best Nine citation. He achieved similar success in the 1998 season, leading the league with 181 hits and a .358 batting average. Because he recorded only 11 stolen bases, his career low for a full season, some people speculated that he had lost enthusiasm for the game. "I didn't lose my desire to play in Japan," he later admitted, "but it wasn't interesting to me anymore."

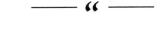

"I was flattered and I wanted to see what they were saying about me, to read it every day," Suzuki said about the publicity he received early in his career. "But I realized I should not have those kinds of feelings. It showed there was something wrong inside me."

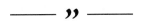

To help provide their star player with a challenge, the Blue Wave sent Suzuki to participate in the 1999 spring training camp with the Seattle Mariners. Suzuki thoroughly enjoyed his time at their facility in Peoria, Arizona. He asked the other players about the strategies they used against major-league pitchers, hoping that he might compete against them some day. He participated in a couple of exhibition games and learned some American slang. Best of all, he enjoyed everyday life in a place where he wasn't famous. He returned to Japan feeling invigorated and confident that Major League Baseball was in his future.

The Blue Wave wanted to keep their star player happy playing in the NPB, so they signed Suzuki to a record-setting contract during 1999. His one-year deal earned him 500 million yen, or almost $4.15 million dollars. Nevertheless, he started the season with a bit of a hitting slump. "When I went after a pitch, just before I hit it I couldn't follow it with my eyes," Suzuki recalled. During this bad streak, a simple groundout provided the mental image he needed to fix his problem. He adjusted the angle of his front foot so that he made contact with the ball at the correct angle. Soon after making this adjustment, he hit his 1,000th career hit, setting a Japanese record by reaching the milestone in only 757 games. By the time an errant pitch broke his wrist and ended his season five weeks early, Suzuki had 141 hits and led the league with a .343 batting average.

Although Suzuki still yearned for the challenge of playing in America, his loyalty to his manager, Akira Ohgi, kept him in Japan for the 2000 season. During the season he came close to his goal of hitting .400, but another injury, this time a rib muscle strain, ended his season in August. He finished with an average of .387, the second-best in NPB history, and earned his seventh consecutive Best Nine and Gold Glove citations. Although he still had one season left before he became a free agent, the Blue Wave allowed him to "post" with Major League Baseball. In the posting system, Japanese clubs auction off the rights to a player to a Major League team, earning a fee for trading their player. Several teams bid for the rights to Suzuki, including the New York Mets and the Los Angeles Dodgers. The Seattle Mariners won the auction with a bid of $13.1 million and offered the outfielder a three-year contract worth more than $15 million. Suzuki was thrilled. "I needed something more for my own love of the game and also to make my fans happy," he explained. "The decision to come to the United States was a natural one so that I could challenge the best in the world."

> "Compared to the pressures I had in the past, this pressure is nothing. When I play in Japan, people expect me to be the leading hitter every year," Suzuki explained. "Even if there are things that become stressful, I think they're interesting. Isn't it because of those things that I am to be struck by the significance of being alive?"

Joining the Seattle Mariners

Suzuki's contract with Seattle made him the first Japanese position player (non-pitcher) to join a Major League Baseball (MLB) franchise. Although his lifetime stats in Japan were impressive—a .353 batting average, with 1278 hits and 199 stolen bases—there were many in the United States who doubted he could make much of an impact with Seattle. They argued that American pitching was far superior to Japanese pitching and that at just 5'9" and 160 pounds, he was too small to hit well in larger American

Suzuki during his first season with the Mariners, 2001.

ballparks. Suzuki didn't listen to naysayers; instead he studied tapes of American pitchers, learned to work with his teammates, and perfected his technique. "Compared to the pressures I had in the past, this pressure is nothing. When I play in Japan, people expect me to be the leading hitter every year," he explained. "Even if there are things that become stressful, I think they're interesting. Isn't it because of those things that I am to be struck by the significance of being alive?"

Suzuki was still the focus of the Japanese media, despite the move to Seattle. Over 150 reporters followed him to America, and his games—even preseason ones—were broadcast live in Japan. Nevertheless, the move meant he could get his hair cut or take his wife out to eat without attracting a crowd.

Suzuki began proving his worth early in the 2001 season. By the end of April, he was batting .333 and the Mariners had set a major-league record by winning 20 games for the month. His teammates nicknamed him "the Wizard" for his speed and skills, while American fans were now the ones shouting "Ichiro" from the stands. He had a 23-game hitting streak during May and June; in July he became the first rookie to lead all players in All-Star voting. He earned a record 3.3 million votes, including half a million internet votes from Japan. Suzuki didn't let up for the rest of the year. He led the league with a batting average of .350 and 56 stolen bases, the first player to lead both categories since Jackie Robinson in 1949. His 242 hits

Suzuki's batting skill continued unabated after he joined the Mariners.

set a new record for a rookie and also made him the first player since 1930 to have more than 240 hits in a season. Suzuki was named American League Rookie of the Year and Most Valuable Player, only the second player ever to earn both accolades in the same year. He also earned a Gold Glove for fielding, committing just one error during 152 games in the outfield.

Aided by Suzuki's incredible rookie performance in 2001, Seattle tied the MLB record for wins in a season with 116 and was headed for the playoffs. In the division series against the Cleveland Indians, Suzuki hit .600, going 12-for-20 as Seattle took three of five games. The Mariners then had to face the New York Yankees in the American League Championship. The Mariners folded against Yankees pitching, and Suzuki's .222 average for the series contributed to the team-wide batting slump as they lost the series four games to one. Although he found it painful to watch the Yankees in the World Series, Suzuki said that "I and my teammates gave it everything we had. We showed our best. Because of this I didn't anguish over the loss for a long period of time." Still, despite his magical rookie season he felt he had more to prove. "[Am I] satisfied? That is a difficult word," he said. "In some aspects of the game, I still have things to do."

In the 2002 season Suzuki started strong, carrying a .384 average into June. At mid-season he again led the majors in All-Star voting with 2.5 million votes. Although he suffered a bit of a slump in September, he still finished the year with a .321 average and 208 hits, second-best in the league. He earned his second consecutive Gold Glove, making only three errors in the outfield. Although Seattle missed the playoffs, in November Suzuki led the MLB All-Stars to victory over the Japanese All-Stars, hitting 4-for-4.

In 2003, his third major league season, Suzuki proved he was just as dependable as he had been in Japan. He played in all but three of 162 games. His 2.1 million All-Star votes led the majors for the third season in a row. Although his season average dipped to .312, that still placed him in the top 20 players in the league. In addition, his 212 hits placed him second in the league, and his two fielding errors earned him a third Gold Glove. And he was still drawing the fans to Seattle's stadium, including thousands of Japanese tourists. Well aware of his value, the Mariners signed him to a contract extension at the end of the year, worth $44 million over four years.

Breaking Batting Records

Suzuki entered the 2004 season feeling he still had something to prove to himself and his fans. He started slowly, taking until mid-May to keep his batting average above .300, and then he became unstoppable. He collected at least 50 hits in the months of July, August, and September, becoming the

Suzuki had a stupendous season at the plate in 2004, including this at-bat on October 1. He's about to get his 258th hit of the season, breaking the previous record by George Sisler of the St. Louis Browns, set in 1920.

first MLB player to ever have three consecutive 50-hit months. By the end of August he had already reached 200 hits, the fastest pace in 35 years. People began talking about the possibility that Suzuki could break one of baseball's oldest records: George Sisler's single-season hits record of 257, set in 1920. Ichiro passed the mark on October 1 and finished the season with a new record of 262 hits. That total included 225 singles, which broke Willie Keeler's major league record from 1898. Suzuki won the 2004 batting title with an average of .372, which set a Mariners team record. As the first player to record 200 hits in his first four seasons, Suzuki also set an all-time major league record for the most hits—924—for a player's first four years, or for any four-year span.

It is difficult for any athlete to follow up a record-breaking season, and 2005 was no exception for Suzuki. While his 206 total hits were second-best in the American League, his season batting average was .303, his lowest yet. Suzuki had hoped to perform better, but he had learned a lesson after his record-breaking run of hits in 2004. "I realized it was impossible to please [everyone]. I discovered I needed to do what I needed to, [and] if people like it, that's good. I became more confident. And that Ichiro became a part of me, instead of me chasing after him," he said. "When people get placed upon a pedestal—when they start chasing after that person on the pedestal—they become mannequin-like. People striving for approval from others become phony. You should seek approval from yourself." Despite the dip in his statistics, Suzuki still became the first player in the majors to record at least 200 hits in first five seasons.

> "
>
> *"I realized it was impossible to please [everyone]. I discovered I needed to do what I needed to, [and] if people like it, that's good. I became more confident," Suzuki clarified. "When people get placed upon a pedestal—when they start chasing after that person on the pedestal—they become mannequin-like. People striving for approval from others become phony. You should seek approval from yourself."*
>
> "

Suzuki returned to form in spring 2006, when he competed for Japan in the first ever World Baseball Classic (WBC). A 16-team tournament featuring the best players from leagues all around the world, the WBC was the first international tournament to include MLB players. Suzuki helped Team

Japan reach the championship game, which they won 10-6 over Cuba. The outfielder was named to the all-tournament team with a batting average of .364; he hit safely in all eight games and got 12 hits in 33 at-bats. He was thrilled to compete for his home country in the tournament. "Apart from the Olympics, I really wanted this WBC tournament to be the event that decides the true world champions, so that's why I participated in this event," he said. "And at the end, I was able to be on the championship team, and this is probably the biggest moment of my baseball career."

Suzuki had little time to rest before the 2006 MLB season began. He had another good year, leading the league with 224 hits and posting a respectable .322 average. He set both Mariners and American League records by stealing 39 bases in a row. Nevertheless, the outfielder felt somewhat discouraged that 2006 was Seattle's third year in a row finishing last in their division. "We've had three years here where we haven't won. It's definitely been hard on me mentally to spend so much time with us losing," he said. There was talk about his contract expiring after the next season and whether he might jump to a team with better prospects. But Suzuki wasn't eager to leave, noting that "Seattle is a special city to me.... I want to be a player who is wanted and needed for the team and for the fans. The fans have always been behind me, and I thank them and appreciate them."

Suzuki and the Mariners were back in form during 2007. In mid-season he signed a contract extension that kept him in Seattle. The five-year contract was worth around $18 million a season, making him one of baseball's top earners. With questions about his contract behind him, Suzuki could focus on performing. In his seventh consecutive All-Star Game, he was named MVP after going 3-for-3 and hitting the first inside-the-park home run in the game's history. Shortly after, he earned his 1500th major league hit. He finished the season with a .351 average, second best in the majors, and led the league with 238 hits, 203 singles (the third highest singles mark in league history), and 44 infield hits. Suzuki hadn't lost his step in the outfield, either, with only one error in 155 games—even though he had switched from right field to center field. He earned his seventh consecutive Gold Glove for fielding excellence and a Silver Slugger award for batting.

Striving for Excellence

A number of elements, both physical and mental, have contributed to Suzuki's triumphs as a baseball player. His success at hitting is a matter of talent and skill, developed through hard work. His opponents marvel at the hand-eye coordination that allows him to consistently put the fat part of the bat on the ball. Infielders respect his speed—half a second faster to

Suzuki's fielding skills are one of the reasons he is considered a superlative player. In his first seven seasons in the major leagues, he played nearly 9,400 innings but only made 15 errors.

first base than the average major leaguer—which forces them to play closer to home plate and allows him to lob more singles past their positions. "The ability to make contact is just how I learned to hit," he explained. "That's been a focus ever since I was a little player. That was important, and so I worked on it." He carefully considers his opponent up on the pitching mound. "When I get up [to bat], I feel and get a sense of the pitcher. I analyze what he might throw me, then I trust my sense of the pitcher and make the adjustment." During games, if he does not place the ball exactly where he planned, he will sometimes watch himself on video replays and then make corrections.

But hitting and offense are only part of Suzuki's skill as a ballplayer. "I cannot be the player I am without defense and speed," he noted. "I cannot impress you only with hitting. Defense and running make me a good player." With his strong defensive skills, opponents rarely try to take an extra base when a ball is hit to him in the field, for fear his rifle-fast arm will throw them out. In addition, he has only 15 errors for his major league career, although he has spent nearly 9,400 innings in the outfield.

Conditioning is also an important part of his game. Suzuki is noted for performing an elaborate stretching routine before every at-bat, and sometimes during downtime in the outfield. He pays attention to fitness during the off-season as well. One year he regularly ran up and down stairs for 90 minutes, logging more than 25,000 steps over 2.5 months. "Actually, I don't know if I'm that disciplined," he remarked. "I only do what my body asks me to—not what my head tells me to do. If I start doing things I don't like, baseball won't be fun anymore."

> "You don't turn in a spectacular performance because you happen to be in supreme condition that day," Suzuki argued. "It's the times when you're in a normal mental state that you have a chance to turn in a great performance. If you allow yourself to drift out of normalcy because of pressure or frustration or some other factor, that's when things can go wrong."

Although he makes the most of his physical skills, Suzuki has said that the mental aspect is the most important part of his game. "You don't turn in a spectacular performance because you happen to be in supreme condition that day," he argued. "It's the times when you're in a normal mental state that you have a chance to turn in a great performance. If you allow yourself to drift out of normalcy because of pressure or frustration or some other factor, that's when things can go wrong." He focuses on specific points in a ballpark before each at-bat in order to "achieve mental control." Then, after a game is finished, he oils and maintains his own glove, which is custom-made in Japan, before storing it in a special cotton bag. "This is not only baseball equipment to me, but they are part of me. You know, parts of my body," he explained. "The goal is to be as close [to perfect] as possible. In order to achieve that, it is imperative to set aside a period of self-reflection daily. That's what the time with my glove represents for me."

Now that he has a new, long-term contract in Seattle, Suzuki noted, he can be the type of player who has "the security he needs to settle down and devote himself entirely to the game.... As long as I can enjoy playing ball I hope to keep playing the way I have been." But he'll continue to try to perfect his game. "I'm surprised at the things I still don't know, which makes me want to keep on playing."

MARRIAGE AND FAMILY

Suzuki began dating television broadcaster Yumiko Fukishima in late 1997, and they married on December 3, 1999. "If it weren't for her there wouldn't be an Ichiro of the Mariners," he said. "My wife's the one who helped make my dreams come true." The two of them live in Seattle with Ikky, their pet Shiba Inu (a Japanese breed of small dog). They reportedly have homes in Los Angeles and Arizona, near the Mariners' spring training camp.

HOBBIES AND OTHER INTERESTS

Suzuki enjoys playing Go, a strategic board game that originated in Asia. He also collects coins, paintings, and exotic Japanese custom cars, and he practices the traditional Japanese art of bonsai, or growing miniature trees. In 2006 he began taping his own Japanese television show, "Ichiro Versus." The program pits him against a prominent figure from another field, such as science, law, fashion, or entertainment, as they talk one-on-one and participate in a psychological test. His favorite part of the program is the word-association game, in which each person says the first thing that comes to mind after hearing a word or phrase. Suzuki enjoys talking with different types of people. "I think it's important to come in contact with people from as many different walks of life as possible. Otherwise, you limit what you can experience and you end up stifling your growth potential."

Suzuki earns about $10 million a year in endorsement deals, including agreements with companies related to sports gear, financial services, oil, drugs, and mobile phones. Although he doesn't often publicize his efforts, he is also very involved with various charities. In Japan he has been involved with the Make-a-Wish Foundation, which helps grant wishes to seriously ill children.

WRITINGS

Ichiro on Ichiro: Conversations with Narumi Komatsu, 2004 (translated by Philip Gabriel)

HONORS AND AWARDS

Most Valuable Player, Pacific League (Nippon Professional Baseball): 1994-1996

Best Nine (Nippon Professional Baseball): 1994-2000

Gold Glove (Nippon Professional Baseball): 1994-2000

Most Valuable Player, American League (Baseball Writers Association of America): 2001

Rookie of the Year, American League (Baseball Writers Association of America): 2001

All-Star Team (Major League Baseball): 2001-2007

Gold Glove, American League (Rawlings): 2001-2007

Silver Slugger Award, American League (Hillerich & Bradsby): 2001, 2007

Players Choice Award (MLB Players Association): 2001, for Outstanding Rookie, American League, and 2004, for Outstanding Player, American League

Commissioner's Historic Achievement Award (Major League Baseball): 2005, for setting single-season hits record

All-Tournament Team, World Baseball Classic: 2006

Most Valuable Player, All-Star Game (Major League Baseball): 2007

FURTHER READING

Books

Leigh, David S. *Ichiro Suzuki,* 2004 (juvenile)

Levin, Judith. *Ichiro Suzuki,* 2007 (juvenile)

Suzuki, Ichiro. *Ichiro on Ichiro: Conversations with Narumi Komatsu,* 2004 (translated by Philip Gabriel)

Periodicals

Baseball Digest, Dec. 2001, p.40; Nov. 2002, p.22; Dec. 2004, p.20

Chicago Sun-Times, May 13, 2001, p.126

Current Biography Yearbook, 2002

Fort Lauderdale (FL) Sun-Sentinel, July 9, 2001, p.C1

Los Angeles Times, Mar. 9, 2001, p.D13

New York Times, May 21, 2001, p.D4; June 9, 2002, p.SP3; Sep. 14, 2004, p.D1; Sep. 5, 2007, p.D4

New York Times Magazine, Sep. 16, 2001, p.50

Seattle Post-Intelligencer, Sep. 29, 2006, p.C1

Seattle Times, Mar. 30, 2007

Sporting News, Mar. 19, 2001, p.12; May 21, 2001, p.22; Mar. 10, 2003, p.10; May 20, 2005, p.14

Sports Illustrated, Dec. 4, 2000, p.68; Apr. 23, 2001, p.36; May 28, 2001, p.34; July 8, 2002, p.50
Sports Illustrated for Kids, Apr. 2002, p.29; Dec. 1, 2004, p.15
St. Louis Post-Dispatch, June 10, 2001, p.F9
Tacoma (WA) News Tribune, July 14, 2007
USA Today, Feb. 21, 2001, p.8C; May 15, 2007, p.C1
Washington Post, May 24, 2005, p.D1

ADDRESS

Ichiro Suzuki
Seattle Mariners
SAFECO Field
1250 1st Avenue South
Seattle, WA 98134

WORLD WIDE WEB SITES

http://seattle.mariners.mlb.com

Photo and Illustration Credits

Cumulative Names Index

This cumulative index includes the names of all individuals profiled in *Biography Today* since the debut of the series in 1992.

For cumulative general, places of birth, and birthday indexes, please see biographytoday.com.

153

For cumulative general, places of birth, and birthday indexes, please see biographytoday.com.

For cumulative general, places of birth, and birthday indexes, please see biographytoday.com.

155

For cumulative general, places of birth, and birthday indexes, please see biographytoday.com.

157

For cumulative general, places of birth, and birthday indexes, please see biographytoday.com.

159

For cumulative general, places of birth, and birthday indexes, please see biographytoday.com.

For cumulative general, places of birth, and birthday indexes, please see biographytoday.com.

165

For cumulative general, places of birth, and birthday indexes, please see biographytoday.com.

For cumulative general, places of birth, and birthday indexes, please see biographytoday.com.

167

Biography Today

General Series

For ages 9 and above

Biography Today **General Series** includes a unique combination of current biographical profiles that teachers and librarians — and the readers themselves — tell us are most appealing. The **General Series** is available as a 3-issue subscription; hardcover annual cumulation; or subscription plus cumulation.

Within the **General Series**, your readers will find a variety of sketches about:

- Authors
- Musicians
- Political leaders
- Sports figures
- Movie actresses & actors
- Cartoonists
- Scientists
- Astronauts
- TV personalities
- and the movers & shakers in many other fields!

"Biography Today will be useful in elementary and middle school libraries and in public library children's collections where there is a need for biographies of current personalities. High schools serving reluctant readers may also want to consider a subscription."
— *Booklist,* American Library Association

"Highly recommended for the young adult audience. Readers will delight in the accessible, energetic, tell-all style; teachers, librarians, and parents will welcome the clever format [and] intelligent and informative text. It should prove especially useful in motivating 'reluctant' readers or literate nonreaders."
— *MultiCultural Review*

"Written in a friendly, almost chatty tone, the profiles offer quick, objective information. While coverage of current figures makes *Biography Today* a useful reference tool, an appealing format and wide scope make it a fun resource to browse." — *School Library Journal*

"The best source for current information at a level kids can understand."
— Kelly Bryant, School Librarian, Carlton, OR

"Easy for kids to read. We love it! Don't want to be without it."
— Lynn McWhirter, School Librarian, Rockford, IL

ONE-YEAR SUBSCRIPTION
- 3 softcover issues, 6" x 9"
- Published in January, April, and September
- 1-year subscription, list price $66. **School and library price $64**
- 150 pages per issue
- 10 profiles per issue
- Contact sources for additional information
- Cumulative Names Index

HARDBOUND ANNUAL CUMULATION
- Sturdy 6" x 9" hardbound volume
- Published in December
- List price $73. **School and library price $66 per volume**
- 450 pages per volume
- 30 profiles — includes all profiles found in softcover issues for that calendar year
- Cumulative General Index, Places of Birth Index, and Birthday Index

SUBSCRIPTION AND CUMULATION COMBINATION
- $110 for 3 softcover issues plus the hardbound volume

For Cumulative General, Places of Birth, and Birthday Indexes, please see www.biographytoday.com.